the
Burden
Bearer

who's carrying your load?

PAUL W.
CHAPPELL

First published in 2012 by Striving Together Publications, a
ministry of Lancaster Baptist Church, Lancaster, CA 93535.
Striving Together Publications is committed to providing
tried, trusted, and proven books that will further equip local
churches to carry out the Great Commission. Your comments
and suggestions are valued.

Striving Together Publications
4020 E. Lancaster Blvd.
Lancaster, CA 93535
800.201.7748

Cover design by Andrew Jones
Layout by Craig Parker
Edited by Monica Bass

ISBN 978-1-59894-213-2

Printed in the United States of America

DEDICATION

To the Burden Bearer

Contents

Acknowledgements   vii

Author's Note   ix

Preface   xi

PART 1: LIFTERS AND THEIR BURDENS

Chapter One—Tipping Points   3

Chapter Two—Giants in the Land   15

Chapter Three—But What If?   31

Chapter Four—Self-Imposed Burdens   45

Conclusion to Part 1   59

PART 2: BURDENS RELIEVED

Chapter Five—Where Burdens Are Lifted   63

Chapter Six—A Better Way   73

Conclusion to Part 2   85

PART 3: SERVING IN CHRIST'S YOKE

Chapter Seven—Learning to Rest   89

Chapter Eight—The Language of Grace   101

Chapter Nine—Leave It to the King   113

Chapter Ten—When Ministry Hurts   129

Chapter Eleven—Depends on How You Look at It   141

Conclusion to Part 3   153

Appendix—The Impossible Burden   155

ACKNOWLEDGEMENTS

ANYONE WHO HAS undertaken the process of writing a book knows that it can be a burden on multiple levels, especially a heartfelt burden to communicate truth. The Lord has recently brought me through a season of learning to cast my cares on Him. As He was teaching me to rely on His strength, I felt compelled to share it in book form. Some of these pages were handwritten in the wee hours of the morning—with you in mind.

I'm grateful to my wife, Terrie, who has encouraged and prayed for me as I've learned and relearned to let Christ bear my load. Terrie, your love and loyalty is beyond what I deserve. I'm thankful that we have the privilege of serving the Lord together.

I'd like to thank my writing assistant, Monica Bass, for implementing the allegory and seeing the manuscript to completion. I also thank Dr. John Goetsch for his work in reviewing and encouraging the development of the allegorical portions of this book.

Finally, I'd like to thank my staff and our church family. Thank you, staff, for helping to bear my burden and the burden of ministry. It is a joy to serve in the yoke with you. Thank you, Lancaster Baptist Church, for cultivating a heart for the Lord and for sharing the burden of the Burden Bearer—a care for souls. It is a privilege to be your pastor.

AUTHOR'S NOTE

DO YOU KNOW the Burden Bearer?

I met Him April 5, 1972—the best day of my life. He took my load of sin, and He became my closest friend.

Strange as it may seem, however, I still find myself burdened. Perhaps you do too.

How is it that we who personally know the One who invites us to cast our cares upon Him still stagger on bearing our own loads?

How is it that we who have chosen Christ's easy yoke persist in carrying our lopsided weights on our shoulders rather than hitching them to our shared yoke with Christ?

How is it that we who have dedicated ourselves to the service of *the* Burden Bearer so often find ourselves feeling heavy, burdened, weighted, and exhausted?

And one more question: If we learn to cast our cares on His shoulders, do we release them from our own?

These are questions that the Lord has been answering in my mind and heart over the past couple of years, and I'd like to share with you what He is teaching me.

Some things are best learned by a story, and so in these pages we meet Carrier—the main character in our burden-bearing allegory. I'm hopeful that the allegorical element of this book will bring a fresh perspective to truths that we sometimes struggle to apply. At the beginning of each chapter, we'll spend a brief time with Carrier and then move to scriptural applications for our lives.

Ultimately, I pray that through these pages we will discover the strength of the Burden Bearer and learn to cast ourselves into His everlasting arms.

NOT LONG AGO and not far away, Mr. and Mrs. Thinkstrong gave birth to their second son. "He's so small," his father declared. "His cry is so weak," his mother lamented. "He's scrawny," the nurse scoffed as she left the room.

Gratified to be alone with his wife, Mr. Thinkstrong looked long and hard into her eyes. "How could this happen? It was so different with his brother. Brawn came into the world ready to take it on. He was born big and strong, and his bellowing cry echoed down the hospital hallways. All the nurses admired him the moment they laid eyes on him."

The Thinkstrongs were born and reared in the village of Lifters. In Lifters, the strongest always won and the smartest always prevailed. If a man didn't pull himself up by his own bootstraps, he didn't get up. There was no coddling in the village of Lifters. The weak were silently (and often not so silently) scorned.

Mr. and Mrs. Thinkstrong's dilemma was obvious. They had brought a weakling into this world of vitality. What were they to do? Was their fate to raise a son who would be the brunt of jokes and the object of every villager's scorn his entire life?

"I know what we'll do," Mrs. Thinkstrong said with sudden inspiration. "As you know, every Lifter is expected to live up to his or her name. We'll give our new son a name to live up to—a name of strength and courage." She looked fondly—and now even hopefully—at the little one nestled in her arms. "We'll call him *Carrier*."

"*Carrier*?"

"Yes—*Carrier*. We will teach him to ponder the meaning of his name and to live a life fitting of his name. We will teach him to carry his own load through life. He'll carry his own load physically, and he will carry his own load emotionally. He will learn to rely on himself. He will strengthen himself every day to grow worthy of his name. I believe it's our only hope—*his* only hope."

"*Carrier* it is," said Mr. Thinkstrong. And so, Carrier it was.

Carrier had plenty of assistance in learning to live up to his name. When as a toddler he fell, his father spoke gruffly, "Get up, Carrier—men don't cry." When he would ask his big brother, Brawn, for help with a project, Brawn would coolly reply, "No, Carrier—Lifters always do it themselves." When he missed a catch or fell behind in a race, his coach would admonish, "Hey, Carrier, show us what you're made of—you'll never make it if you don't try harder. Now, get going!" When Carrier received a C on his report card, his mother corrected, "This is not a grade befitting of a boy named *Carrier*. Try harder, Carrier—try harder." Or at least, these were the words Carrier heard.

Carrier's family wasn't harsh; they also spoke words of encouragement to him. But they did want Carrier to succeed, and they knew that his only hope was strength. In fact, to really understand a Lifter, you have to know that *all* of them had the words *try harder, try harder* running through their minds like a script. It was the unwritten motto of Lifters. Try harder.

On the day a Lifter took his first step, he received a Pack. "Start them early," the villagers had always said as they strapped the Pack to their tiny tot's back. A Lifter's Pack became a badge of honor. Obviously, a full Pack meant he could carry a heavier load. Every Lifter wanted a full Pack. The really brave ones made sure they had *overflowing* Packs, and the really vain ones imitated the really brave ones. For the most part, everyone had Packs that were heavier than they should have been carrying.

And that is why they needed the Burden Bearer.

Strange thing, however, about the Lifters who knew the Burden Bearer: some of them went right on carrying their loads by themselves—as if they didn't really know the Burden Bearer at all. Of course, those who knew the Burden Bearer had already given Him their loads of Sin (see page 155), but many of them seemed to think that was all He wanted to carry for them—at least that's what you would think if you saw them staggering through Lifters under their loads.

Carrier was one of these Lifters—one who knew the Burden Bearer but who still carried his own load. True to his mother's predictions and his father's dreams, Carrier had learned to live up to his name. And he courageously loaded his Pack full. And fuller. And fuller.

Not to shock you but Lifters actually is *your* hometown, and Carrier actually is *you*! Like Carrier, we are born into a world of burdens—a world where the strongest win, and the weak are crushed beneath their loads. We have family burdens, financial burdens, relational burdens, emotional burdens, health burdens, work burdens, responsibility burdens, and yes, even ministry burdens.

Some of us carry our burdens by natural capacity—some are simply stronger than others. Others of us do it by strategic management—learning how and when to conserve and expend energy. But even the strongest grow weary, and the smartest meet their limits. "Even the youths shall faint and be weary, and the young men shall utterly fall" (Isaiah 40:30).

And so, we all need the Burden Bearer—Jesus Himself.

To all who will hear, our Burden Bearer calls, "Come unto me, all ye that labour and are heavy laden, and I will give you rest" (Matthew 11:28).

Strange thing, however, about us "lifters" who know the Burden Bearer: we still have burdens. Stress. Fear. Anxiety. Perfectionism. And more. And stranger still, we often go right on carrying our loads all by ourselves—even though we know *the* Burden Bearer.

Carrier's story—which is not so unlike our own—is meant to remind us that there is a better way, that Jesus invites us to cast *all* of our burdens upon Him.

Who's carrying your load?

> *But they that wait upon the LORD shall renew their strength; they shall mount up with wings as eagles; they shall run, and not be weary; and they shall walk, and not faint.*—ISAIAH 40:31

PART ONE

Lifters and Their Burdens

Cast thy burden upon the Lord, and he shall sustain thee: he shall never suffer the righteous to be moved.—PSALM 55:22

God resisteth the proud, and giveth grace to the humble. Humble yourselves therefore under the mighty hand of God, that he may exalt you in due time: Casting all your care upon him; for he careth for you.—1 PETER 5:5–7

CHAPTER ONE

Tipping Points

CARRIER PAUSED TO shift the load in his Pack. Actually, as long as Carrier could remember, he had been shifting loads. It was a key strategy he had learned as a weak youngster. And it seldom failed him now.

Burdens readjusted, Carrier continued walking; and as he walked, he reflected on how thankful he was to know the Burden Bearer. In fact, Carrier had chosen some years ago to serve the Burden Bearer, and some of the loads in his Pack had actually come *from* the Burden Bearer. Of course, Carrier still had some of his own loads as well—the kind of loads common to all Lifters—Mortgage, Job, Difficult Boss, etc. And, like other Lifters, he had some invisible loads as well—Tension, Worry, Fear, and Grief.

But lately, Carrier had begun to notice a frightening difficulty. No matter how much he shifted the weights in his Pack, he was becoming less able to carry it. Just that morning, as he had been getting ready for work, he noticed in the mirror that his shoulders were stooped, his energy was short, and his perspective was heavy.

What's wrong with me? Carrier questioned himself as he trudged to work. *I'm supposed to be growing stronger, not weaker.*

Carrier thought about each of the loads in his Pack. He thought about the loads he was carrying for the Burden Bearer. He shifted them around in his mind. But no matter how he looked at them or repositioned them, he couldn't seem to make even one of them lighter.

So he ignored the strain and trudged forward.

Just ahead, Carrier saw his good friend Bestrong, and he hurried to catch up.

Always fresh and energetic, Bestrong greeted Carrier with a slap on the back, or rather a slap on the Pack.

"How's it going, Carrier?"

If any other Lifter had asked this question, Carrier would have forced a smile (hoping it appeared more genuine than it was) and said "great" with more enthusiasm than he felt. But Bestrong had been his closest friend for years. They had met at Recharge—a place where all the Lifters who knew the Burden Bearer met weekly.

"Actually," Carrier began, "I don't know what to do." And he sat down on a sidewalk bench in exhaustion.

Bestrong sat down next to Carrier, his energy softening into sympathy. "What's wrong?"

"I just can't do it all," Carrier said bluntly. And he hung his head in shame. That was a tough confession for a Lifter.

"That's right," Bestrong said encouragingly.

Carrier looked up in surprise. Maybe Bestrong hadn't heard him correctly. He rephrased his confession with different words. "My load is too heavy. I can't go on like this much longer."

"No, you really can't," Bestrong agreed.

Carrier was surprised—and a bit irritated—at Bestrong's calm responses. How could he so easily say, "No, you can't do it all"?

The two sat in silence for a few minutes until Bestrong spoke. "I'm really glad to hear you finally say it, Carrier."

Carrier was getting frustrated. "Glad?!"

"Yep. I know it's tough to say, but it's the first step to getting help."

"Yeah, really? Like from who?"

"The Burden Bearer."

Carrier snorted. "You don't understand, Bestrong. Half of my load of Stress relates to what I do for the Burden Bearer!"

"The source of your Stress is inconsequential. Wherever your Stress comes from or whatever it's made of, the Burden Bearer is really good at bearing it."

"Easy for you to say, Bestrong. You're always equal to the load in front of you—that's why we call you Bestrong!"

"Really? What if I told you that Bestrong was just the beginning of my name?"

Carrier looked at his friend with curiosity.

"It's really long, but I've shortened it for my friends. Altogether it is BeStrongInTheLordAndInThePowerOfHisMight."

Carrier laughed, and the relief felt good.

"Seriously," Bestrong continued, "I learned a long time ago—about the time that I was crushed under my load of stress—that I don't have the strength to be strong on my own. I can only do it in the might of the Burden Bearer." He paused and then added, "I had what you might call a tipping point."

I began studying lever and fulcrum physics when I was four. And I didn't even use a textbook. (Actually, I couldn't read yet.) My education came via the playground.

It didn't take me long to learn that if I was at the bottom of the teeter-totter, and my younger, lighter sister was at the top, I could give her a fast crash landing by simply getting off my seat. I may not have fine-tuned the exact tipping point, but I knew it was there, and before I even knew what it was called, I could leverage it to my advantage.

Our lives are a little bit like that playground teeter-totter, in that we have tipping points. Physically, emotionally, spiritually, relationally—we reach a point when our equilibrium is catapulted off balance and we find ourselves in a free fall.

The culprit?

Stress.

What's tipping your balance?

Stress adds spice to life. Think about it. A life with no stress would be void of victory or conquest. It would be empty of suspense and challenge. We need stress—it's a good thing.

But as helpful as some stress may be, we do have a tipping point.

Too much stress is like being on the heavy side of the teeter-totter. You can't get off the ground no matter how hard you try. Except perhaps for a brief jump that expends all of your energy.

Dr. Richard Swenson calls too much stress *overload.* In his book *Margin,* he cites areas of overload that burden our lives.[1] Individually, we may be able to manage any one of them. But collectively? We don't have enough time, energy, or emotional strength to continually juggle them all.

- Activity Overload
- Change Overload
- Choice Overload
- Commitment Overload
- Debt Overload
- Decision Overload
- Expectation Overload
- Fatigue Overload
- Hurry Overload
- Information Overload
- Media Overload
- Noise Overload
- People Overload
- Possession Overload
- Technology Overload
- Traffic Overload
- Work Overload

Stress has become an epidemic. The American Stress Institute reports that stress is responsible for 250 million lost workdays per year.[2] Additionally, 75–90 percent of all doctor visits are for stress-related complaints.[3] It is estimated that American companies spend at least $300 billion annually due to stress-related accidents, absenteeism, and attrition as a result of workplace stress.[4] According to the National Institute of Mental Health, more than 23 million Americans suffer from some form of anxiety disorder.[5]

While everyone lives with some level of stress, there can be no doubt that we live in a day when stressors have reached debilitating levels in many Christians' lives. Among full schedules, heavy demands, and never-ending urgencies, we easily find ourselves in a chronic state of depletion with no reserve.

We may be able to handle some stress on our own, but we do have a tipping point. Once you've passed yours, the burden of stress becomes unsustainable.

Bring it on

Many of the stressors you and I experience are unique to our period in history. Or at least the sheer volume and speed at which they pile on is unique to our unrestrained age of progress.

But stress itself is not new. Neither is overload. It's a common burden Christians of all ages have carried in their Packs.

No doubt Elijah had reached his tipping point when he collapsed under the juniper tree and requested death (1 Kings 19:4). He had just confronted King Ahab about his sin, conducted a spiritual showdown of massive proportions, personally executed 450 false prophets, and had been chased out of town with a price on his head. Talk about stress!

Martha knew something of stress. In Luke 10:40 we find her frustrated under the load of her service. "But Martha was cumbered about much serving, and came to him, and said, Lord, dost thou not care that my sister hath left me to serve alone? bid her therefore that she help me." In today's terms, we might say that Martha was "stressing out." The frazzling details of her day had exhausted her patience and pushed her near her tipping point.

The major stressors that enter our lives are often not of our own choosing. They may be laid on our shoulders through decisions or events outside our control. Sometimes they pile so high that we really don't believe there is an answer or a way to escape the load.

When these trying circumstances enter our lives, we must accept God's assignment and believe that He has a sovereign plan. That's not an easy task, but questioning God or being angry at Him does not help us bear the burden of stress. It weakens us and moves us nearer to the tipping point.

The greatest stress in my life, to this point, has been watching my oldest son, Larry, endure two surgeries and intense chemotherapy during his battle with cancer. While God has been gracious and Larry's recent tests have revealed good results, even today the thought of Larry's pain or his upcoming tests produce an increased stress level. My heart begins to race, my blood pressure rises, and a deep tension headache sometimes sets in.

In fact, there was a day when an accumulation of stressors pushed me to a tipping point of physical collapse. With my blood pressure at 220/115, I realized that I needed to learn a better way to handle the burden of stress.

I trusted God, but I had reached my tipping point.

Room to tip

Tipping points aren't all bad. They can be used of the Holy Spirit to bring positive change into our lives.

One of the most significant principles I learned at my tipping point was the principle of margin. To again quote Dr. Swenson, "Margin is the space between our load and our limits. It is the amount allowed beyond that which is needed. It is something held in reserve for contingencies or unanticipated situations. Margin is the gap between rest and exhaustion, the space between breathing freely and suffocating."[6]

When you are living with no margin and are always in "overload mode," a major stressful event can become a tipping point. Living with margin provides room to tip before you reach the tipping point.

Consider Elijah. When he collapsed under the juniper tree, he was absolutely wrung out—physically, emotionally, and spiritually. What if he had held his emotions in check and planned some time for personal rest and refreshment before conceding failure? As it was, the Lord intervened and restored the margin Elijah had lost. God fed him and gave him forty days to regain his equilibrium.

Consider Martha. She missed the spiritual margin that comes through worship, and as a result, her service became overly cumbersome. Had she followed Mary's example and spent time at Jesus' feet, she would have had a clearer perspective of her to-do list.

Consider yourself. Have you allowed margin to replenish your batteries so you are not chronically running on reserve power?

Under the cape

Before we can adequately understand the solution to overload, we need to first answer the question, "Why are we in overload anyway?" Why have we, like Carrier in the parable, determined that high levels of stress are normal?

Stress is obviously related to the fact that we are over-extended in some area—most commonly our schedules and commitments. But what is the root issue of this complex? Why do we don the Superman (or Superwoman) cape in the first place?

There could be many answers to that question, some of which we'll look at in chapter 4. But I speak for myself and, I have discovered, for a host of other Christians sincerely wanting to do more for Jesus. Long before the overloaded schedule, the migraine headaches, or the fatigue, there was a willingness to "surrender all" to Jesus.

But then we began to lose our equilibrium.

Somewhere in the process of our busy schedules, we forgot the surrender-all-to-Jesus mindset and we developed a do-it-all-for-Jesus philosophy. One problem. Jesus never created—nor expects—us to do it all. In fact, He will never equip us to do it all.

I have taught church leadership across America and around the world for two decades. I believe in and practice the principles I have taught:

- People do what people see; leaders must set the example.
- People only respect what we inspect; leaders must manage the process.
- We must regulate what we delegate; leaders are responsible to follow through.

The list goes on. As you can see from these points, I believe in being fully engaged in causative leadership. I believe in follow through, and I believe the Christian's life should reflect order.

Yet, as I enter the second half of my life, the Lord is also teaching me that I don't have to fix every problem.

I don't have to do God's job.

I can take off the Superman cape.

To be sure, I have always known and preached that the church is the Lord's. And I still work with intensity and passion as a pastor. I would never encourage a spiritual leader to become a slacker in the work of God. But there is a difference between being lazy and giving the burden of stress to the Lord.

Your stress burdens may look different from mine. They may be primarily attached to your job, your relationships, your schedule, your goals, your finances, your ministries, or a host of other variables. They are likely a combination of several burdens. But whatever the stress burdens in your Pack look like, I challenge you to build margin into your life. Outside of uncontrollable emergencies (which come to everyone and are part of the reason that we *need* margin), be unwilling to carry more stress than fits in your Pack when you are not wearing your Superman cape. The Burden Bearer did not design your body or your mind to carry an unrestrained burden of stress.

We do not need good Christians falling out of the race because of over-extension and hyper-stress. In America alone, stress-related illness costs billions of dollars each year to treat, and consecrated Christians are no exception to the symptoms and treatments of stress-related maladies.

Removing the cape and creating space to breathe is a means by which we acknowledge to the Lord that we are not able to bear the burden of stress without Him.

The overcomer's secret

One of the truths the Lord used in my life to lift the load of stress from my shoulders is summed up in this statement: A sacrificial life will always be unfinished. (Yes, this means that I won't finish everything today.)

There is a fine line between diligence and drivenness. At least on the surface. Underneath, there is a chasm. Driven Christians carry the stress of trying to do God's work for Him. Diligent Christians fully give themselves to the Lord and trust Him to do His work through them.

Ultimately, if the Lord doesn't build the house (or the Sunday school class, or the church, or the family, or the business, or the relationship, or _____), we are laboring in vain anyway

(Psalm 127:1). We release the burden of stress when we release the responsibilities for the outcome to the Lord.

You don't have to wait for a stress-induced tipping point. You don't have to run until your legs are crippled with stress fractures. You don't have to add more stress burdens to your Pack until your shoulders are permanently stooped.

Yes, in this world there is unavoidable tribulation. But the Lord has already overcome this world and bids us to follow His lead, to ride in His wake, and to be an overcomer.

You can drop the cape.

You are an overcomer through Christ.

---

1. Richard Swenson, *Margin: Restoring Emotional, Physical, Financial, and Time Reserves to Overloaded Lives* (NavPress, 2004), 61–63.

2. The American Institute of Stress, "Workplace Stress" (accessed October 24, 2012), http://www.stress.org/workplace-stress/.

3. Joseph Goldberg, "The Effects of Stress on Your Body (July 23, 2012), http://www.webmd.com/mental-health/effects-of-stress-on-your-body.

4. The American Institute of Stress, "Workplace Stress" (accessed October 24, 2012), http://www.stress.org/workplace-stress/.

5. Archibald Hart, *The Anxiety Cure* (Thomas Nelson, Inc., 2001), 7.

6. Richard Swenson, *Margin: Restoring Emotional, Physical, Financial, and Time Reserves to Overloaded Lives* (NavPress, 2004), 69.

CHAPTER TWO

Giants in the Land

AFTER CARRIER'S TALK with Bestrong, he felt a sense of relief—he could finally breathe again. He was still overloaded with the burdens in his Pack, but he now knew where they belonged—in the Burden Bearer's hands. With a skip and a whistle, he started home to share Bestrong's advice with his wife, Carryitall.

Carrier's steps slowed considerably when he noticed the long shadow crossing his path ahead. He hesitated, weighing his options for escape. But he didn't have to wait long, for Giant Terror met him before he had decided what to do. Once they stood face to knee, Carrier couldn't move an inch—his feet were firmly fixed as if they had their own Packs holding them down.

"Well, well, we meet again," Terror sneered.

"Yep, looks like we do," Carrier's attempt at lightness ended in a decidedly nervous titter.

"Still have my load?" Terror demanded with a chilling squeeze to Carrier's shoulder.

It had long been a puzzle to Carrier why a strapping giant like Terror couldn't carry his own burden, but that seemed to be the case. Every time Terror met Lifters, he heaped them up with a load of Fear, demanding they carry it for him. Carrier's load had grown through the years and was becoming so heavy that it seemed to weigh on his very soul.

Fear was a strange burden—as if it were a *living* burden. Big, bulky, and cumbersome, it found ways to reach through his Pack searing straight through his back and squeezing his heart in its icy grip.

Especially troubling to Carrier was that he knew Fear had consumed so much space and weight in his Pack that there was less room to effectively manage his other burdens. Sometimes, because of Fear, he even had to tell the Burden Bearer "no" when He asked Carrier to assume another burden. How Carrier wished he could rid himself of Fear! But with Giant Terror lurking about and stalking him, that didn't seem likely.

"I hate to trouble you, little Carrier," the Giant snarled, breaking off Carrier's thoughts, "but I have more Fear for you to carry. See, it's just too heavy for me." And with that, he dumped a heavy load into Carrier's Pack and slunk away.

"I just can't...." The words were not yet out of Carrier's mouth when the Burden Bearer appeared.

Carrier sat down quickly, hiding his Pack from the Burden Bearer. The Burden Bearer sat next to him.

"What's in your Pack, Carrier?"

Somehow, Carrier realized that the Burden Bearer already knew. "Fear," he mumbled.

"Do you want to keep it?"

That seemed like an odd question to Carrier. Of course he didn't want to keep it! What Lifter would actually *want* to lug around a load of Fear? "I don't have a choice," he returned.

The Burden Bearer smiled. "You do have a choice, Carrier. But you will not see the choice until you *want* to see it."

Carrier wasn't so sure he wanted to see the choice. What if it was a difficult choice? What if it was a choice that required all his energy? And worst scenario of all, what if it required that he pull Fear out of his Pack to see his choice? Heavy as Fear was, Carrier had learned long ago that it was easier to carry it than to face it.

But the Burden Bearer was still waiting for an answer.

"I think," Carrier fairly choked out the words. "I think…well, I think that I do want to see the choice."

The Burden Bearer smiled again. "Good. It's actually quite a simple choice."

Carrier sighed with relief. "Whew! I was afraid it was going to be hard."

"Oh, but it sometimes is hard. There's a difference between simple and easy."

"I see," Carrier responded, wishing he hadn't seen.

"Carrier," the Burden Bearer paused until Carrier looked up and met His gaze, "do you believe Me?"

Carrier squirmed. "Of course I believe You. You took my load of Sin, and You've never failed me." But somehow he knew that wasn't quite what the Burden Bearer was asking.

"Would you believe anything—everything—I tell you?"

Carrier looked away. *Everything? What if it was hard to believe? What if it was harder to believe than to carry Fear?* But when Carrier looked back at the Burden Bearer, he knew his answer. No one could look directly into those soul-encompassing eyes and answer anything but, "Yes…everything."

"Would you believe Me if I told you that I can take your Fear?"

"Yes."

The Burden Bearer was obviously pleased with Carrier's answer. "It's just that simple, Carrier."

"As simple as saying 'yes'?"

"As simple as believing My word." And with that, the Burden Bearer reached into Carrier's Pack and pulled out the heavy burden of Fear.

"See," He said, "It's not even heavy to Me. There's no reason for you to carry it any longer."

With Fear exposed in the Burden Bearer's hands, it didn't look nearly as frightening as Carrier had imagined it might if *he* had ever dared to pull it out. In fact, it looked quite puny.

Carrier now laughed out loud in the face of Fear. "Burden Bearer, I believe You. I believe anything You say…everything!"

"I am certain that my fellow Americans expect that in my induction into the Presidency, I will address them with a candor and a decision which the present situation of our Nation impels."

A nation strapped with the financial burdens of the Great Depression listened eagerly to their new president's inaugural address.

"This is preeminently the time to speak the truth, the whole truth, frankly and boldly. Nor need we shrink from honestly facing...."

President Franklin Roosevelt continued while listeners stood in the chilly wind by the East Portico of the Capitol and others strained to listen through their crackling radios. The new president hadn't spoken five whole sentences before he made a statement which the nation would remember for years to come: *"The only thing we have to fear is fear itself."*

You've probably heard this statement more than once. And you've probably encountered the reality of its topic more than that. What Christian who is determined to move forward for the Lord hasn't felt the clammy burden of fear strapped to his back and weighing his steps...or prohibiting progress altogether?

I've carried the burden of fear far more times than I'd like to admit. And I can never seem to get rid of it on my own. But every time I face it in the light of God's promises, I'm reminded just how puny it is compared to the faithfulness of my God.

One of my favorite portions of Scripture when I am facing fear is the account of the Israelites' entry into the Promised Land. With one failed attempt followed by an overwhelmingly successful attempt forty years later, we can learn much about the paralyzing effect of fear and the triumph of faith in God's promises.

Fear itself

For ten of the twelve spies Moses sent to scout out the land of Canaan, "fear itself" strikingly resembled the giants they saw towering in the plains.

After a miraculous delivery from slavery in Egypt, the Israelites had traveled across the wasted wilderness toward Canaan—the land which God had promised them.

The journey was filled with faith, and the journey was filled with doubt. Mostly doubt. It seemed every day that doubt found reasons to voice its fear. Sometimes with a whine and sometimes with a voice of true terror, the Israelites repeatedly questioned, "Can God?" "Will God?"

But God was gracious to the Israelites, and He led them on. Finally, they came to the very brink of victory—the shores of Jordan itself. Moses chose twelve men and commissioned them to scout out the land across the river. Their observations would be crucial in the nation's strategy of conquest.

Grapes and giants

The twelve spies were overwhelmed by the bounty of the land. God had told them it was a good land, but never in their wildest dreams could they have conceived that it was *this* good!

Near Hebron, in the Valley of Eshcol, the men cut a giant cluster of grapes so heavy it necessitated two men carrying it suspended from a pole between them. The remaining men carried colossal pomegranates and succulent figs. Herdsmen by trade, they quickly noticed the rich grazing lands and knew their flocks would multiply quickly. Indeed, this was a land of bounty.

But there was one problem: a giant problem—as in, a problem of giants. These Canaanites were of colossal stature, and they were seasoned warriors. The spies beheld them in terror…and beat a path home.

Fear settled in as the spies carried their heavy grapes and their heavier report back to the Israelite camp.

Improper ratios

The nation assembled to hear the spies' report. What did they see? And what was their suggested strategy for taking the land?

The spies gave the good news first: "We came unto the land whither thou sentest us, and surely it floweth with milk and honey; and this is the fruit of it" (Numbers 13:27). Can you hear the gasp of an entire nation as the spies lifted the two-man cluster of grapes and emptied the pomegranates and figs from their bags? Surely anticipation surged through the waiting people.

"Nevertheless," the spies continued. And with that solitary word, they deflated the optimism of every Israelite. "The people be strong that dwell in the land, and the cities are walled, and very great: and moreover we saw the children of Anak [giants] there" (Numbers 13:28).

The nation began to tremble. "We can't do it," they said to each other. "We're weak; the giants are big."

Caleb tried to settle the nation and renew the people's courage: "And Caleb stilled the people before Moses, and said, Let us go up at once, and possess it; for we are well able to overcome it" (Numbers 13:30).

Back and forth the debate went—ten spies rousing fear and two spies rallying faith.

In desperation, the kind of desperation that comes when fear has an iron grip on your mind, the ten spies declared, "And there we saw the giants, the sons of Anak...and we were in our own sight as grasshoppers, and so we were in their sight" (Numbers 13:33).

Like *grasshoppers*? Really?

That's an incredible ratio when you think of it. Let's say the average Israelite soldier stood five feet eight inches tall. Even a very large grasshopper would stand about one inch tall. For the Israelites to be like grasshoppers to the Canaanites, the giants would have to be approximately 385 feet tall.

Fear is irrational. It makes us see our problems bigger than they really are, and it makes us see our own resources smaller than they really are. Most of all, it absolutely blinds us to the power of God and the faithfulness of His promises.

When fear has so bent your back that you are reduced to the height of a grasshopper, it's time to release the burden.

What are your giants?

I don't know what giants may have pushed their way into your life, but I've cowered under the shadow of a few. And they're all intimidating.

Maybe you're facing the giant of financial instability. Or emotional oppression. Or family struggle. Or ministry defeat.

Giants have an uncanny ability to grip your heart in a vice of fear and squeeze out your joy. They are experts at flaunting their height and reminding you of your weakness.

But as imposing as giants may be, they all flee before one Defender—God.

And our powerful God sends the giants packing in response to one choice on our part—faith.

Faith makes a difference

While the Israelites moaned in defeat, two men held fast to their faith. "And Joshua the son of Nun, and Caleb the son of Jephunneh, which were of them that searched the land, rent their clothes: And they spake unto all the company of the children of Israel, saying, The land, which we passed through to search it, is an exceeding good land. If the LORD delight in us, then he will bring us into this land, and give it us; a land which floweth with milk and honey. Only rebel not ye against the LORD, neither fear ye the people of the land; for they are bread for us: their defence is departed from them, and the LORD is with us: fear them not" (Numbers 14:6–9).

How's that for a nation-motivating speech? Those are words that rekindle faith and stir hope.

But the Israelites had already *chosen* fear, so they didn't hear a single word Joshua and Caleb so valiantly articulated. Instead "all the congregation bade stone them with stones" (Numbers 14:10).

Thankfully, Moses stepped in and stopped the stone slinging, but the people lost the land. Because the giants were bigger to them than their God, they wandered in the wilderness for forty years until every one who chose fear was dead. Their children would be the ones to slay the giants—under the leadership of Joshua and Caleb. Because these two men believed God was bigger than the giants, they were the only men of their generation to enter the Promised Land. And the only difference between them and the others was the choice of faith over fear.

Fear busters

What caused Joshua and Caleb to hold faith when the rest of the nation caved in to fear? What could equip two men out of two million people to believe in God when every visible evidence—including stones flying in their direction—indicated that the way ahead was impossible?

Could their secrets help us to let go of the burden of fear and send our giants packing?

These two men possessed two secret weapons that conquered their fears and equipped them to triumph in faith.

A sword for every giant

Joshua and Caleb knew that God had given His word to Moses that they would posses the land. In fact, possession was the very reason Moses had obeyed God's instructions to send out spies in the first place. "Send thou men, that they may search the land of

Canaan, which I give unto the children of Israel…" (Numbers 13:2). And many years earlier, God had given His word to Abraham that He would give the land to Abraham's descendants (Genesis 12:1–3).

Armed with these two promises, Caleb and Joshua were sure of God's intent to give them the land.

Our faith, too, is strengthened by God's Word. Romans 10:17 tells us, "So then faith cometh by hearing, and hearing by the word of God." D.L. Moody once said, "I prayed for faith and it did not come, but when I read the Word of God, then faith came."

Ephesians 6:17 instructs us to take "the sword of the Spirit, which is the word of God." There is no weapon like God's Word. So why don't we grab it when we first hear the giant's footsteps approaching? If you want to release the burden of fear, you must search out and claim the promises of God's Word.

Are you struggling with fear of insufficiency? Claim Philippians 4:19, "But my God shall supply all your need according to His riches in glory by Christ Jesus."

Are you struggling with fear of inadequacy? Claim Isaiah 41:10, "Fear thou not; for I am with thee: be not dismayed; for I am thy God: I will strengthen thee; yea, I will help thee; yea, I will uphold thee with the right hand of my righteousness."

Are you struggling with fear of tomorrow? Claim Jeremiah 29:11, "For I know the thoughts that I think toward you, saith the LORD, thoughts of peace, and not of evil, to give you an expected end."

Are you struggling with fear of failure? Claim Philippians 2:13, "For it is God which worketh in you both to will and to do of his good pleasure."

Are you struggling with fear of rejection? Claim Ephesians 1:6, "To the praise of the glory of his grace, wherein he hath made us accepted in the beloved."

Are you struggling with fear of loneliness? Claim Hebrews 13:5, "Let your conversation be without covetousness; and be content with such things as ye have: for he hath said, I will never leave thee, nor forsake thee."

Are you struggling with fear of exhaustion? Claim 2 Corinthians 12:9, "And he said unto me, My grace is sufficient for thee: for my strength is made perfect in weakness. Most gladly therefore will I rather glory in my infirmities, that the power of Christ may rest upon me."

Are you struggling with fear of fear itself? Claim 2 Timothy 1:7, "For God hath not given us the spirit of fear; but of power, and of love, and of a sound mind."

When we neglect God's Word, we lose sight of what God not only *desires* to do, but what He *can* do in our lives. Like an unused muscle, our faith begins to atrophy. On the other hand, when we feed our souls on God's promises, our entire perspective changes. Although we are aware of our weaknesses and the impossible circumstances surrounding us, these are not our focus. Our focus is God's limitless power.

God has provided a sword to defeat every giant. But it is up to you to seek it out and to wield it in faith.

A power for every need

Behind the Word of God is the power of the Holy Spirit Himself. No one else can give us strength to face our fears.

The Holy Spirit empowered Joshua and Caleb to respond to the giants, not with fear, but with a spirit that trusted God. Of Caleb, God said, "because he had another spirit with him, and hath followed me fully, him will I bring into the land whereinto he went; and his seed shall possess it" (Numbers 14:24).

These two men had a believing, trusting spirit that boldly declared, "the LORD is with us: fear them not" (Numbers 14:9).

They knew that it was God's power that would lead them to victory. Thus, they had nothing to fear.

As Christians, we, too, have access to the mighty power of God. Where our ability fails, His might defeats the giants. Hebrews 13:6 encourages us, "So that we may boldly say, The Lord is my helper, and I will not fear what man shall do unto me."

We need a spirit that holds fast to God's promises and claims His power. That is precisely the renewing spirit referred to in Ephesians 4:23, "And be renewed in the spirit of your mind." A Christian who is walking in the flesh never has the right spirit. He is quenching the indwelling Holy Spirit and is unable to know the victory that the Holy Spirit brings over fear.

Caleb and Joshua "wholly followed the LORD" (Joshua 14:8). When all others were controlled by their fears, these men were governed by the Holy Spirit of God. They remained dedicated and devoted to their Lord. When we are equipped with the power of the

Holy Spirit, we will respond in the same believing, trusting spirit as Caleb and Joshua.

The spoils belong to the faithful

Fast forward forty years. Once again, Israel camped on the bank of the Jordan. Once again, the leader (who is now the faithful Joshua) sent spies into Canaan.

Wisely deciding to not repeat history, Joshua sent out only two spies. The spies likewise chose to leave history buried in its defeat. Having learned from the faith of Caleb and Joshua, they returned with a good report: "Truly the LORD hath delivered into our hands all the land; for even all the inhabitants of the country do faint because of us" (Joshua 2:24).

During the forty years Israel had wandered in the wilderness, nothing much had changed in Canaan. The giants hadn't shrunk. The Israelites hadn't grown taller. Then why the adjusted report? What gave these spies this remarkable courage? The change had sprung up in the hearts of God's people. Where they had miscalculated their ratios, they now claimed victory in the strength of their Lord.

But for two of the Israelites, there was a special blessing. Because Caleb and Joshua had faced the giants with faith and then held fast their faith for forty years, God gave them the privilege of securing for future generations the inheritance of the Lord. Joshua led the nation to conquer the land. And Caleb? Even to his eighty-fifth birthday, he was eager to lead the way by faith. He asked for an entire mountain, and Joshua gave it to him. "And they gave Hebron [where forty years earlier he had hoisted grapes onto a pole] unto Caleb, as Moses said: and he expelled thence the three sons of Anak" (Judges 1:20). The giants still were no match for Caleb's faith. He conquered every last one of them.

Release your load

Is fear gripping your heart? Has a foreboding giant strapped a heavy burden to your shoulders and commanded you to carry it?

Drop the burden. Trust in the power of God to carry you.

We have nothing to fear but fear itself. Faith or fear—the choice is yours.

CHAPTER THREE

But What If?

"CARRIER, WHAT'S HAPPENED to you? You look so… well, so…I don't even know what to call it." The shocked expression on Carryitall's face betrayed her surprise.

"Light?"

"Yes, I guess that's it. Your Pack is obviously lighter, but it's your face, too. I haven't seen you looking this relaxed in years. What's going on?"

So Carrier relayed to his wife the day's encounters—his conversation with Bestrong and his meeting with the Burden Bearer. Carryitall listened quietly. A woman well known for getting things done and seeing responsibilities through, this was a new way of thinking to her.

"I wish I could lighten my load like you did yours," she finally admitted when Carrier finished.

"You can! And why don't you?"

"My Pack is full of things you don't understand, Carrier. Bestrong taught you to lighten your Pack from Stress. The Burden Bearer led you to give Him your Fear. But my load is different from yours—my Pack is mostly filled with Worry. To be sure, Worry does keep Stress with it, but that's different from your Stress burden."

Carrier wasn't sure what to say. Since the previous events of the evening, he was convinced that the burdens in his Pack—or for that matter in Carryitall's Pack—weren't as indispensable as he had previously believed. On the other hand, he still had quite a few burdens in his own Pack, so it wasn't like he was an instantaneous expert at load-dropping.

"Plus," Carryitall added, "Worry can actually be a *helpful* burden. It reminds me of all the details in my responsibilities, and it keeps me on my toes. Take for instance the twins' birthday party I'm planning for Saturday. And the ladies luncheon at church I'm coordinating next month…and our Christmas plans with our extended family (you know, so many of them don't know the Burden Bearer, and I want us to be the very best testimony, so it all has to go perfectly)…and then there are the test results from the doctor that I'm waiting for…." Carryitall began to choke up here. Obviously this Worry was close to her heart.

Carrier put his arms around his wife. "I know, Sweetheart, you do have a full plate and many causes for Worry."

Carryitall relinquished her struggle to hold back her tears. "It's not so easy to let go of it all as you think," she cried. And then she released great sobs that had been restrained for too many days.

"Fear might be easy to boot out of your Pack," she continued, "but Worry is different. It's broken up in little loads, and it's persistent."

"But there's one thing I'm not understanding," Carrier said, apparently not having heard his wife's last comment. "Why did you say that Worry is a helpful burden? It seems to me that it's more of a sabotaging burden. Doesn't it weigh you down as you're trying to execute your responsibilities? If you had no Worry in your Pack, wouldn't it free your mind to do all the things you're so capable of?"

"No Worry in my Pack," Carryitall sniffled dreamily. "It sounds so good, Carrier. But I don't think it's possible. I just can't help wondering about *what if*. What if the twins' party is a disappointment to them?"

"I know," Carrier interrupted. "You are concerned and involved about the details of everything. What if the ladies don't come to the luncheon? What if the speaker doesn't communicate well? What if a stray hair makes it into the food?"

Carryitall laughed at her husband's last question—it was just like him to try to lighten her worry with humor. But then she sobered. "Carrier, what if the doctor calls and says that the test is positive?" Her voice lowered, "What if there's no cu—"

"Hey, remember, we're trusting the Burden Bearer about the test," Carrier interrupted. "Don't waste your energy wondering if your condition is treatable when you don't yet even know what your condition is!"

"I know, you're right. But that's easier said than done. It's just that my Pack's always full of Worry. It's there when I get up in the morning, it torments me all day long, it keeps me awake at night, and it even pushes its way into my dreams. I just can't get it out of my Pack."

"I'm new at this myself, Carryitall," Carrier spoke, rubbing his temples in brain exhaustion. "But I do know this much—with the Burden Bearer, there *is* a better way."

"Well, in the meantime, will you help me blow up the balloons for Saturday?"

"Of course." Carrier was thankful to divert their discussion into action.

"I think I left them on the porch," Carryitall said as she opened the front door. She reappeared in a moment with the balloons and a puzzled look on her face. "Look, here's an extra balloon with a note."

> *Carryitall,*
> *Put this in your Pack. It will help.*
> *~The Burden Bearer*

"What does it mean?" Carryitall asked. How can *adding* to my Pack help? Not that this light, deflated balloon is going to make much of a difference."

"Look," Carrier pointed out, "the balloon has words on it."

"But they're too scrunched to read," Carryitall returned, scrunching her own face in hopes of making out the words.

"Maybe we're supposed to blow up the balloon so we can read the words before putting it in your Pack."

"My Pack's already full—there's no way that balloon will fit if it's blown up."

Ever the strategist, Carrier suggested, "I'll put it in your Pack before I blow it up, and then I'll see how much air it will hold."

As Carrier filled the balloon, a surprising result unfolded, or rather, unpacked. Something in that balloon's make-up enabled it to maneuver the air inside it underneath the loads of Worry and to lift those loads up and out of the Pack. By the time the balloon was full, all the Worry had overflowed out of Carryitall's Pack, leaving only the balloon in her Pack.

Carrier and Carryitall stood astonished as they surveyed the now homeless loads of Worry spread across the floor. Then Carryitall laughed out loud. And she laughed again, and again, and then Carrier laughed with her. He caught his wife's hands, and they danced about the room.

"Wait," Carryitall stopped in the middle of a step. "We forgot all about the writing on the balloon—what does it say?"

Carrier looked into his wife's Pack. "It says 'PRAISE.'"

"Praise? Yes, that makes perfect sense when you know the Burden Bearer. When I fill my Pack with Praise, there is no room left for Worry. Whoever knew it could be that simple!"

"But remember," Carrier said, echoing words the Burden Bearer had spoken to him a few short hours earlier, "simple doesn't always mean easy."

Somewhere between Palm Springs and Phoenix I saw a billboard that startled me. Actually, it challenged me. It even changed me.

The sign was from our homeland security department, and it read, "We can be afraid, or we can be ready."

I was startled for two reasons. First, because the government had a message that made perfect sense! Second, because in the midst of a tremendous season of trials and worry, the sign convicted me that I had not been more well-equipped for the attacks and trials of life.

After all, I am a pastor. I tell people every day how to bear their burdens. But problems can mount and become personal in a moment's time. As I drove, I realized I wasn't ready for all I was facing. And worrying about the trials wasn't helping.

We know the admonition of Scripture: "Be careful for nothing" (Philippians 4:6). And yet, we tend to be full of care for many things. Like the loads in Carryitall's Pack, worry fills our minds and hearts, leaving little space for God's peace or God's power to aid us. In reality, worry is a sin—a lack of faith in God's Word. And the resulting burden of this sin includes sleeplessness, body twitches, high blood pressure, and broken health. I know from experience.

Worry brings a load of care that we simply are not strong enough to carry.

Stronger arms

Thankfully, we are not left to shoulder our own burdens. We have a God greater than every "what if" of life. And He is willing to assume our load. "The eternal God is thy refuge, and underneath are the everlasting arms" (Deuteronomy 33:27). Our Burden Bearer will carry our worries, if we will only entrust them to His keeping. Release from worry has nothing to do with release from trouble. Rather, release from worry comes when we cast our worries on the Lord and receive His peace to face our troubles.

In 1554, Nicholas Ridley was sentenced to be burned in Oxford, England, at the stake for the "heresy" of preaching that salvation is through Christ alone. After twenty long months of torturous imprisonment, the eve of his execution had finally arrived. Amazingly, Nicholas appeared stronger than those nearest him. When the prison-keeper's wife delivered his supper, he noticed she was weeping for him. Almost cheerfully, he thanked her for supper with the words, "Though my breakfast will be somewhat sharp, my supper will be more pleasant and sweet."[1]

It is said that on this same evening, Nicholas' brother offered to stay with him in prison, hoping to be a comfort to him. "It is not necessary," Nicholas replied. "I mean to go to bed and sleep tonight as quietly as ever I did in my life." Ridley intimately knew the peace of God, and it gave him rest in the refuge of the everlasting arms.

God's peace is always available for His children. Isaiah 26:3–4 promises, "Thou wilt keep him in perfect peace, whose mind is stayed on thee: because he trusteth in thee. Trust ye in the LORD for ever: for in the LORD JEHOVAH is everlasting strength." The perfect peace promised in this passage comes to those who keep their minds fastened on the Lord, resisting the very real temptation to worry about their past, present, or future circumstances.

Sufficient supplies

When we worry, we fret that we are not enough, that our resources are inadequate, that the demands on us are overwhelming, that eventually, we will be unable to sustain the pressures and burdens we are carrying.

Charles Spurgeon once told of an evening when he was riding home, weary and depressed, after a heavy day's work. Suddenly, 2 Corinthians 12:9 flashed through his mind: "My grace is sufficient for thee." He said, "I should think it is, Lord," and burst out laughing. He said that it seemed to make unbelief so absurd. It was as though some little fish, being very thirsty, was troubled about drinking the river dry, and the river said, "Drink away, little fish, my stream is sufficient for thee." Or, it seemed after the seven years of plenty, a mouse feared that it would die of famine, and Joseph might say, "Cheer up, little mouse, my granaries are sufficient for thee." Or, a man away up on a mountain saying to himself, "I fear I shall exhaust all the oxygen in the atmosphere." But the earth might say, "Breathe away, oh man, and fill thy lungs ever; my atmosphere is sufficient for thee."[2]

The Christian need never carry the burden of worry. God is sufficient to meet our needs, and His strength is able to carry our burdens.

A surprise source of strength

In Philippians 4:6–8 (the same passage that instructs us to "be careful for nothing") God gives a fourfold directive for releasing the burden of worry.

You might think that the first step in resolving your worry is to solve your problems. But actually, it's something entirely different. It begins with the simple (although not always easy) directive, "Rejoice in the Lord alway: and again I say, Rejoice" (Philippians 4:4).

Worry is misleading. Somehow we feel that by meditating on our difficulties and their possible negative outcomes, we are preparing ourselves for what lies ahead. In reality, these mind exercises diminish our ability to deal with today. As Corrie ten Boom, the Christian author and Ravensbrück concentration camp survivor, pointed out, "Worry does not empty tomorrow of its sorrow; it empties today of its strength."

Praise, on the other hand, has the opposite effect. Praise refocuses our hope on God Himself and thus renews our spirit, providing courage to face whatever circumstances lie ahead. Nehemiah pointedly and simply testified, "the joy of the Lord is your strength" (Nehemiah 8:10).

Notice from Philippians 4:4 that God doesn't command us to rejoice only when we *feel* like it. He commands us to rejoice *always*—no matter what our inner feelings or outer circumstances may be.

How can we rejoice when life's dark clouds surround us and the future looks foreboding? To rejoice is a choice. And when the object of our rejoicing is the Lord Himself, we can make this choice regardless of our circumstances.

God is *always* good. God is *always* present. God is *always* faithful. God is *always* greater than whatever we face. Therefore, we can *always* rejoice in Him.

The Lord is at hand

Remembering God's presence gives us a poise that worry does not know. Philippians 4:5 says, "Let your moderation be known unto all men. The Lord is at hand."

Dr. Lee Roberson once told the story of a young husband whose wife had died, leaving him with their small son to rear alone. The evening of his wife's funeral, the father took his son to bed with him early, hoping to escape his aching loneliness through sleep. But the little boy was restless and confused. Every few minutes, he would break the silence with a heart-rending question, "Daddy, where's Mommy?" or "Daddy, when is Mommy coming back?"

Finally, after several still moments, the child reached out in the darkness toward his father's face. "Daddy," he asked, "is your face toward me?" Satisfied that his father was near and watching him, he readily fell asleep.

We may face moments when we are tempted to fear that God has forgotten or forsaken us, and those are the moments when we worry and fret. But God's face is always toward His children; there is nothing that can separate us from His love.

> *Who shall separate us from the love of Christ? shall tribulation, or distress, or persecution, or famine, or nakedness, or peril, or sword? As it is written, For thy sake we are killed all the day long; we are accounted as sheep for the slaughter. Nay, in all these things we are more than conquerors through him that loved us. For I am persuaded, that neither death, nor life, nor angels, nor principalities, nor powers, nor things*

present, nor things to come, Nor height, nor depth, nor any other creature, shall be able to separate us from the love of God, which is in Christ Jesus our Lord.—ROMANS 8:35–39

You can rest. His face is toward you. Always.

Anxiety ends where faith begins

Too often, we chide ourselves for worry while we neglect the most powerful release from worry's grip—prayer. With the same stroke of ink that Paul penned "Be careful for nothing," he continued: "but in every thing by prayer and supplication with thanksgiving let your requests be made known unto God" (Philippians 4:6).

The God-given release from the burden of worry is prayer—faith-filled prayer that is so confident in God it utters thanksgiving with its very requests.

George Müller said it this way: "The beginning of anxiety is the end of faith, and the beginning of true faith is the end of anxiety." Faith and anxiety are not compatible. And faith is encouraged to grow when we lift our worries to the Lord in prayer with confidence in His goodness.

Why tomorrow is bright

It has been said that faith in God makes great optimists. And God Himself encourages this belief. In Ephesians 3:20, He points out that He "is able to do exceeding abundantly above all that we ask or think, according to the power that worketh in us."

Adoniram Judson believed in God's ability. The first foreign American missionaries, Judson and his wife Ann took the Gospel to Burma (modern day Myanmar), but they weren't received by people eager to hear the Gospel. For six years, the Judsons labored, seemingly without fruit as they had not one convert for all their effort. After ten years in the country, they had seen just eighteen people trust Christ and follow Him in believer's baptism. It was slow going, but the couple pressed on for the Lord.

But when the Anglo-Burmese War broke out in 1824, Adoniram was mistaken for an Englishman and imprisoned in miserably inhuman conditions. His ankles were tied to a bamboo pole from which he was suspended, only his head and shoulders remaining on the ground. Lying there in the vermin-ridden death jail with over thirty pounds of chains binding his ankles, a fellow prisoner sneered, "Dr. Judson, what about the prospect of the conversion of the heathen?" Judson's instant reply was, "The prospects are just as bright as the promises of God."

Judson's faith was rewarded. When he and Ann had embarked for Burma, his goal was to translate the Bible and plant a church, which he hoped would grow to one hundred members. When he died, he left the translated Bible and over one hundred churches with a combined total of more than eight thousand members.

Indeed, tomorrow is bright because of the promises of God. It's brighter than our darkest fears. It's brighter than our most rehearsed worries. It's brighter than our present circumstances. It's as bright as the very promises of God!

Why is it, then, that we fret when we have the omnipotent power of God intervening on our behalf? Romans 8:31 asks the rhetorical question, "If God be for us, who can be against us?"

And yet, our own minds are bent toward worry. For this reason, Philippians 4:8 instructs us to retrain our thinking: "Finally, brethren, whatsoever things are true, whatsoever things are honest, whatsoever things are just, whatsoever things are pure, whatsoever things are lovely, whatsoever things are of good report; if there be any virtue, and if there be any praise, think on these things."

The final directive in God's cure for worry brings us full circle. Only as we continually choose to rejoice in the Lord will we keep our minds stayed on that which is true and godly. Philippians 4:8 thinking releases our minds from worry's shackles.

Bigger than you think

Have you ever noticed that worry often starts as a light load but grows heavier the longer you carry it?

God notices, too, and He longs to unburden us of these loads. He provides us with a fourfold directive that enables us to lay down the unbearable burden of worry: rejoice in Him, remember His presence, request His help, and rest in His truth.

When we follow these instructions, we not only release a burden that is heavier than we can carry, but we receive a benefit that is greater than we can imagine. Tucked into God's instructions for releasing worry is a promise for those who follow them: "And the peace of God, which passeth all understanding, shall keep your hearts and minds through Christ Jesus" (Philippians 4:7).

Too often, we carry the burden that surpasses our strength rather than resting in the peace that surpasses our understanding. God's peace offers a protection greater than our homeland security department can ever promise. It guards our hearts and our minds and lets them rest in the everlasting arms of Jesus Christ. Now that's security!

---

1. John Foxe, *Foxe's Book of Martyrs* (Hendrickson Publishers, 2004, first edition published in 1563), 300.

2. William Williams, *Personal Remembrances of Charles Haddon Spurgeon* (Passmore and Alabaster, 1895), 25.

CHAPTER FOUR

Self-Imposed Burdens

EVERY LIFTER'S PACK contained a common burden. Soon after each tiny Lifter toddler received his personal Pack, he placed in it his first burden—the same first burden placed in every Lifter's Pack. Some added the burden immediately, some waited several weeks or even years. But by adulthood, there was no doubt it was tightly wedged into the bottom of each Lifter's Pack.

Probably because this burden was such an early weight, Lifters often didn't even remember it was there, weighing down their Packs. But forgetting didn't make it go away. This burden became more tightly consolidated—and bigger—as the years passed.

Carrier himself forgot about this burden. It wasn't until he had disposed of his Stress, Fear, and Worry burdens that he even remembered this brick-like weight that had been given a free ride in his Pack for years. But now, as Carrier examined this long-time burden, he noticed it appeared to be quite similar to the burden of Fear. With surprise, Carrier realized this burden—his first burden— had been molded and shaped by the other burdens he had carried for so long. And at the same time, it had been a sort of "foundation burden," providing his other burdens with support and a platform for existence. Its very density and position in the Pack sustained the weight of the burdens heaped upon it.

Then Carrier remembered. He had first carried this burden many years previous, to impress his grandfather Stout. Smiling wryly, he remembered how gratified he had felt when his Grandpa Stout had admired his carrying this load that was just beyond his strength. "Good job, Carrier! Keep up that tenacity, and you'll really make every Lifter envious."

So Carrier kept that tenacity up.

And up.

And up.

Sometimes he did it for his family; sometimes he did it for his boss; sometimes he did it for his church; sometimes he just did it because it had become a way of life. But whatever the case, he *always* strained beyond his limits. And he *always* strained to hear someone's affirming, "Good work, Carrier, keep it up!"

Meanwhile, this burden at the bottom of his Pack grew heavier and heavier, and more and more compact. Now, with a clear perception of this burdensome weight, Carrier realized it wasn't worth carrying.

Carrier strained to pull the burden out of the Pack. Three words imprinted on the side of the burden gripped his attention:

Fear of Man. Strange as it may seem, Carrier even heard the burden speak to him: "Try harder, Carrier, try harder," it said—over and over again.

No sooner had Carrier laid the burden down when the Burden Bearer appeared. "Come with Me, Carrier," He smiled. "I want to show you something."

"You might as well face it. Glenn's gonna be an invalid for the rest of his life."

It was overhearing just that statement that confirmed in young Glenn's mind that he was *not* going to be an invalid. A few weeks earlier, seven-year-old Glenn's legs and feet had been so badly burned in a fire that the doctor had recommended amputation. Glenn's family refused—at least for the time being—but his burned legs filled with infection. The fire had taken all the flesh from his knees and shins as well as all the toes on his left foot. His transverse arch was destroyed. The doctor said that he would never walk again—not with those legs.

From the bedroom where Glenn was confined, he could hear his mother's friend trying to help his mother face reality—"Glenn's gonna be an invalid for the rest of his life." But Glenn wasn't so sure. In fact, he was determined he would not be. And hearing his mother tell her friend that Glenn *would* walk again strengthened his own resolve.

Glenn and his family did more than talk. They worked. With loving tenacity, they continued to change Glenn's burn dressings and cut away the rotting flesh to clear up the infection. They massaged the little bit of muscle and sinew that remained on his legs. And they prayed.

For Glenn's part, he continually pushed himself past the limit of pain as he asked for this care and willed himself to fight against the searing pain. While in his wheelchair one day, he threw himself out of his seat onto the grass in the back yard, and with his arms he drug his body over to the fence. From there, he gritted his teeth and slowly stood on his charred, lifeless legs. Using the fence as a crutch, he pulled himself along one post at a time—walking for the first time since the accident.

From that moment, there was no stopping Glenn. With resolute persistence, he learned to walk without aid, and then he tried running. Soon, he found that it was less painful to run than to walk, and so he ran everywhere he went. He ran so well, in fact, that at the age of twelve he raced the best high school runners in his area and won.

Glenn's legs remained deeply scarred for life. The loss of his toes and his arch meant that he would never run smoothly, but what he lacked in grace, he made up for in strength and endurance. With a steel determination that won him the title "Iron Horse of Kansas," Glenn Cunningham set a world record as a miler.

How was this possible? How did a young boy with lifeless legs become the world champion—not only setting a record time for running the mile, but inspiring millions of others with handicaps to push forward?

The answer is twofold. In Glenn's own words: "by the grace of God, I learned to run again." His life verse was Isaiah 40:31, "But they that wait upon the Lord shall renew their strength; they shall mount up with wings as eagles; they shall run, and not be weary; and they shall walk, and not faint."

The other reason Glenn ran again was because he imposed the discipline on himself to push through searing pain. His determination and perseverance won the victory. Glenn *chose* to assume the agony of walking and then running. No one could have made this decision for him, but himself.

Pushing through pain

Like Glenn Cunningham, every successful person will impose goals on himself or herself to achieve a cause, improve personally, or even help others.

Self-imposed burdens are often applauded in our society—and rightly so. We marvel at the amount of exercise put forth by a football player like Jerry Rice or the number of free throws shot in practice by Michael Jordan. We encourage our children to diligently and faithfully practice in music, sports, and academics, reminding them that their persistence will pay off.

In the Christian life, too, we press forward. The Apostle Paul wrote, "I press toward the mark for the prize of the high calling of God in Christ Jesus" (Philippians 3:14). And indeed, Paul *did* press. He shared much of what he pressed through in 2 Corinthians 11:23–28.

> *...in labours more abundant, in stripes above measure, in prisons more frequent, in deaths oft. Of the Jews five times received I forty stripes save one.*

Thrice was I beaten with rods, once was I stoned, thrice I suffered shipwreck, a night and a day I have been in the deep; In journeyings often, in perils of waters, in perils of robbers, in perils by mine own countrymen, in perils by the heathen, in perils in the city, in perils in the wilderness, in perils in the sea, in perils among false brethren; In weariness and painfulness, in watchings often, in hunger and thirst, in fastings often, in cold and nakedness. Beside those things that are without, that which cometh upon me daily, the care of all the churches.

When most of us would have fallen out of the race, Paul dug in and doggedly kept going for the Lord. The love of Christ constrained him to give every ounce of his life to the Lord.

Christ is worthy of our all—our greatest effort and highest goals. He is worthy of us pouring our hearts and souls into love-based service for Him. There is no sacrifice that is too great to make for Christ. There is no cause that is greater to live for than that of the glory of God.

The dark side of growth

There are, however, self-imposed burdens with a dark side. These burdens produce exertion of stress levels that to the outside observer seem noble, but in the heart of the one who is pursuing and pushing, there is an emptiness and fear that is not indicative of happy giving. It is the outcome of a dark and lonely process of seeking acceptance and approval that never seems to come.

Indeed, many of our admired heroes and conquerors in the political, religious, athletic, and business realms are running their races out of fear. And it is not the fear of the Lord. It is, in fact, the fear of man.

Driven people often live in the constant shadow of a figure whom they desire to please or from whom they seek approval. Not being aware (at least not aware at a heart level) of the approval and acceptance a believer has in Christ, they live with a constant desire for such a feeling from others. The approval may be something they missed receiving from an absent, angry, or abusive father; or it may be something they need or desire from peers or competitors.

Sometimes this approval drive—this dark, self-imposed burden—breeds an insecurity that causes men and women to become critical of their friends from whom they actually desired such approval in the first place. Their hope having been deferred, they now live and make decisions from a sickly heart. They are unable to rejoice with those who rejoice and seem indifferent to many who weep.

Quit trying harder

From the day we were born, we heard (consciously or subconsciously) "try harder." It was the answer to everything. Failing a class in school? Study harder. Missed a free throw for the basketball team? Practice harder. Not meeting your boss's expectations? Work harder. Family falling apart? Try harder. Harder. Harder. Harder.

But what about when "harder" doesn't work? What about when we're already giving 130 percent? What about when the harder we try, the further behind we fall? What about when we're too exhausted to carry the self-imposed burden any longer?

There is hope for souls bearing the burden of unfound approval and unmet expectations. There is freedom from comparison, guilt, and self-imposed bondage. Your hope is not found in a new set of goals or in trying harder. Your hope is found in comprehending the work of the cross and living in the vital awareness of God's limitless grace.

Arm-chair Lifters

There's no one who has the potential to drive a self-conscious Lifter harder than a critic who thinks he knows how to do it better than the one who actually *is* doing it. We'll call them arm-chair Lifters.

Constructive criticism is, of course, an incredible asset. Even so, it can be a tough pill to swallow. Proverbs 27:6 says, "Faithful are the wounds of a friend...." Some of the most helpful advice and counsel I have ever received has come in the form of such "wounds." As tough as constructive criticism may be, it's helpful if we respond to it properly.

But then there's destructive criticism. Not only is it unhelpful; it is deeply painful, and it can be incredibly damaging to the work of God. (Perhaps this is part of the reason why there are so many verses in Scripture concerning our words and our tongues.)

From time to time, every Lifter who is in the service of the Burden Bearer will have detractors. Unjust criticism is a common issue for any leader trying to accomplish something of value.

Because both constructive and destructive criticism are painful, it is easy to discard criticism that would help us, dismissing it as off-target and faulty.

But of greater danger than misdiscerning criticism is *carrying* criticism. When arm-chair Lifters hand us their bag of criticism, they do it with the assumption that we'll carry it. And most often we do.

I used to. I would listen carefully to people who told me I was too soft or too hard or too _____ (fill in the blank from 10,001 other words that have been offered). Some critics blast my motives. Some seek to fulfill a personal agenda. Some are just simply discontent people. And of course, some actually do help.

I've learned in recent years, however, that I do not have the capacity to listen to and respond to all criticism. And I especially don't have the capacity to *carry* the criticism.

In fact, the Lord has often convicted me when I'm wincing under criticism and impulsively beginning to respond (either to clear my name or to satisfy the critic that I've followed through on his concern) that this is a symptom of pride. Why would the criticism bother me if I were dead to self? As Dr. Lee Roberson used to advise, being dead to self means that we are "dead to criticism and dead to praise."

The burden of criticism is really just the burden of the fear of man in another form.

I'm learning now to ask the Holy Spirit to help me filter criticism for that which He knows would be helpful to me or to the ministry and to let the rest go. It's too heavy a burden for my shoulders.

Liberation

When it comes to running the race God has set before us, neither pain nor personal inconvenience nor critics are our greatest enemies. Rather, our greatest enemies are wrong motives.

Pain is sustainable when we have a reachable goal on the other side. Fear of man, however, is never sustainable, for the targeted goal is constantly moving. Those who run their races for the approval of others will be constantly running—never able to finally cross the finish line.

The only way to break out of this cycle of hopeless running is to find your acceptance in Christ. Whether or not you cross your self-imposed finish line, whether or not you gain the human approval you long for, whether or not you win the applause of your peers—you are accepted in Jesus Christ. Period.

Why do we strive for acceptance that has already been provided in Christ? The Scriptures are clear that "he hath made us accepted in the beloved" (Ephesians 1:6).

Such striving must cease. Indeed, it *will* cease in the heart of the maturing Christian. Living life as though the total outcome is up to me is living a life of slavery. We enslave ourselves to the goals and dreams we've attached to our hopes of man's approval. This slavery kills joy and numbs our souls.

True liberty is found in the emancipation of self thought and in doing the will of God from the heart. We must learn to follow God "as dear children" who bask in the approval of an accepting Father (Ephesians 5:1). When we turn from self thought, we are free to glory in the Father's love and divine purposes. When we strive for fleshly purposes or with fleshly motives, we are robbing ourselves of the blessing of knowing Him. When we desire advancement and growth of our business, church, or family for selfish purposes, we lose the opportunity to truly honor Him.

When we have travelled with such misappropriated motives, we must adjust our course and live to know and enjoy Christ more than the momentary attention of men. In doing this, we choose spiritual joy and peace, and we discover contentment.

A passion that rests

Paul lived with passion—passion for God, passion for the souls of men, passion to run the race Christ set before him to the very finish line.

But Paul also knew rest.

And he knew passion and rest simultaneously because his passion was fueled not by a desire for man's approval, but by the faith of Jesus Christ.

I am crucified with Christ: nevertheless I live; yet not I, but Christ liveth in me: and the life which I now live in the flesh I live by the faith of the Son of God, who loved me, and gave himself for me.
—GALATIANS 2:20

Paul lived by the faith of the Son of God. The faith that he was complete in Christ. The faith that Christ would live through him. The faith that God was working in him. The faith that gave Paul a hunger to experience the daily presence of God. The unsatisfied faith that could rest only in the fullness of God.

An oxymoron?

You have to experience it to know it.

Listen to the coach

Do you long to drop your self-imposed burdens? Do you desire to carry only those loads that the Burden Bearer gives and sustains?

Consider the runner who in his passion to win develops a full regimen of exercises that ends up being counterproductive to his coach's plan of training. This is what many of us do when we impose personal burdens that relate to our passion for human approval—even for our own approval. Sometimes we commit ourselves to doing the wrong exercises for the wrong reasons.

Discipline is vital to the Christian life. But sometimes we must step back and ask the tough questions: Why am I willing to carry this load? And for whom am I bearing it? Is it for God's glory? Or for mine?

The loads we impose on ourselves to please our own egos or to impress our peers are never worth the pain they produce. They're like the misdeveloped runner's exercises. The loads we accept for God's glory are always worth whatever pain or discipline accompanies them.

Whose load are you carrying? And why?

CONCLUSION TO PART 1

THE TYPES OF burdens Lifters carry are as varied and numerous as the Lifters themselves. The specific burdens in your Pack are no doubt unique to your personality, background, culture, family, and countless other variables. Stress, Fear, Worry, and Self-Imposed burdens are simply a few of the most prominent—and, incidentally, those that I have personally struggled with the most. But those we've covered in these pages don't scratch the surface of those available for us to pick up.

Yet, the basic truths we've seen in these chapters are the same, regardless of what burdens you carry in your Pack.

Our Burden Bearer did not design our shoulders to be continually stooped and our backs habitually laden with burdens.

He has invited us to cast every burden on Him—to entrust every one of them to His care.

> *Cast thy burden upon the LORD, and he shall*
> *sustain thee: he shall never suffer the righteous to*
> *be moved.*—PSALM 55:22

Before you proceed to the next chapter, please take a moment to identify the burdens you are carrying. What keeps you awake at night? What seizes your mind first thing in the morning? What concerns raise your heart rate when they come to your mind?

Relief is as simple as casting your burden on the shoulders of the Burden Bearer. He really does care for you.

> *Casting all your care upon him; for he careth for you.*
> —1 PETER 5:7

Personal Reflections

_____

_____

_____

_____

_____

_____

_____

_____

PART TWO

Burdens Relieved

I am crucified with Christ: nevertheless I live; yet not I, but Christ liveth in me: and the life which I now live in the flesh I live by the faith of the Son of God, who loved me, and gave himself for me.—GALATIANS 2:20

Come unto me, all ye that labour and are heavy laden, and I will give you rest. Take my yoke upon you, and learn of me; for I am meek and lowly in heart: and ye shall find rest unto your souls. For my yoke is easy, and my burden is light.
—MATTHEW 11:28–30

CHAPTER FIVE

Where Burdens Are Lifted

CURIOUS REGARDING THE Burden Bearer's destination, Carrier began to silently speculate as they journeyed together. Maybe the Burden Bearer had noticed that he had so emptied his Pack of damaging burdens that He was going to fill it with a different kind of burden—perhaps a large burden to carry for the Burden Bearer Himself.

The more Carrier considered it, the larger (and more desirable) such a burden grew in his mind. Surely this would be a larger load than Carrier had ever had the capacity to carry for the Burden Bearer before. After all, since Carrier had rid himself of Stress, Fear, Worry, and Man-Centered Motives, had he not freed space in his Pack for a very *large* load that he could carry for the Burden Bearer?

As it is often difficult to distinguish between a compelling love-based desire to serve the Burden Bearer and a prideful desire to be entrusted by the Burden Bearer with a larger-than-previous load, Carrier's quiet dreams unconsciously lured him toward a prideful desire. Ever eager to prove his love to the Burden Bearer, Carrier subconsciously geared himself for what was ahead with the old script that was ever ready to replay itself in his mind—"Try harder, Carrier, try harder; you can handle this."

Carrier's thoughts were interrupted by a dark, imposing shadow. As Carrier and the Burden Bearer rounded the corner, Carrier saw it clearly—a large, ugly, blood-stained Cross.

"Remember when you were here before?" The Burden Bearer's gentle voice reminded Carrier of the best day of his life.

"Yes, Burden Bearer. It was here that you took my load of Sin." Then, surveying the great heaps of burdens piled around the Cross, he added, "and the same burden for countless other Lifters."

"Are they all the same burden, Carrier?"

Carrier looked at the Burden Bearer with surprise. "Well, of course," he was about to say, but the Burden Bearer smiled and looked back toward the burdens. Following His cue, Carrier walked closer to get a better look. His surprise turned to shock as he saw his own burdens of Stress, Fear, Worry—and many others he had learned to give to the Burden Bearer—piled around the Cross. "You...You put them *here?*" he stammered.

The Burden Bearer laughed His great, rippling laugh. "Did you think I took your burdens from you because *I* needed them? Of course I put them here. I bore every one of these burdens right here at this Cross a long time ago. I was just waiting for you to hand them over so I could place them where they belonged."

Carrier was quiet for a long time. Surges of emotion and waves of thought flooded his mind as he processed the scene before him. Overriding every feeling and thought was a renewed and deeply enlarged gratefulness. Carrier had known since his first visit to the Cross that the Burden Bearer had paid an unfathomable sacrifice to take his burden of Sin, and he had been grateful. But now, Carrier stood face to face with the fresh, overwhelming reality that the Burden Bearer had, all along, been willing to take the other burdens as well.

But Carrier's gratefulness was bittersweet. He also felt a sense of sorrow for having so long staggered under these loads when the Burden Bearer had already made provision for him to lay them down. He grieved as he recalled, even in recent days, having reached for these already-handed-over burdens again. They were just so familiar, and walking without them was a new way of life that was taking Carrier more time than he would have thought necessary to learn.

Mingled with the gratefulness was a faint sense of confusion—a confusion that could almost be defined as "awe." All along, Carrier had thought that the Burden Bearer *wanted* him to carry these loads, that the more loads he carried, the more service he was doing for the Burden Bearer. But now he saw that the Burden Bearer didn't want him to carry them at all. And yet, Carrier *did* still want to serve the Burden Bearer. What did it all mean?

"Carrier," the Burden Bearer broke into his thoughts. "I don't just want your burdens; I want your Pack as well."

My Pack? Panic surfaced in Carrier's heart. *My Pack is me! It represents my capacity, my strength, my willingness to serve. It practically gives me reason to exist as a Lifter!*

Carrier looked dubiously at the Burden Bearer. "You w-w-want my Pack?"

"Yes." And He reached out His hand.

Carrier's gaze fixed on the Burden Bearer's outstretched hand. The wounds he saw there almost involuntarily drew Carrier's eyes to the Cross. How could he say no to *Him?* How could he deny anything—even his Pack—to the one who had borne Carrier's every burden on the Cross?

Still, conflict prevailed in Carrier's confused heart. How *could* he give up his Pack? His identity? Himself?

Carrier shifted his weight from one foot to the other while he struggled inwardly. Finally, without a word, he dropped his shoulders back and let his Pack slip down his arms. Then he handed it to the Burden Bearer.

The familiar smile spread across the Burden Bearer's face.

The question in Carrier's heart found itself on his lips. "But, Burden Bearer, how will I carry my load now?"

"You'll leave all your loads at the Cross. You no longer need to maintain a capacity for your own burdens. I've already carried them."

"But, but, what about the loads I carry for *You?*"

"Ah, yes, *those* loads." The Burden Bearer paused and looked directly into Carrier's eyes. "I never wanted you to carry a Pack. I have a better way."

Several weeks ago, as I drove onto our church campus, two men positioned in the steel beams of a cross facing our campus entrance caught my eye. Each was in a "cherry picking bucket" as he labored in the lofty spaces of our new construction site. These workers' position "in the cross" was unintentional; but it was a visual I will never forget.

The men's physical position "in the cross" is a picture of our spiritual position "in Christ." And just as their position was a reality—not something they were hoping to achieve—so our position in Christ is a spiritual reality—not something for which we continually strive.

Several months ago, the Lord worked such a paradigm shift in my heart concerning the importance of the cross and of knowing what it means to be in Christ, that I changed my life verse to Galatians 2:20: "I am crucified with Christ: nevertheless I live; yet not I, but Christ liveth in me: and the life which I now live in the flesh I live by the faith of the Son of God, who loved me, and gave himself for me."

From the moment of salvation, the Christian life is to be a life of unity and union with Christ. And all of this is possible because of what happened on the cross.

Where burdens are released

At the cross of Jesus, our sin was paid for—completely. In full. Those of us who know Christ as our Saviour and have received His gift of salvation rejoice in the simplicity of the Gospel. We joyfully rest in the knowledge that our burden of sin was lifted at the cross (see page 155).

But what about our other burdens? What about the ongoing burdens that come from living in a fallen world? What about the burdens of Stress, Worry, Fear, Anxiety? What about poor health and joblessness? What about high bills and empty bank accounts? What about family strife and straying children? What about broken relationships and shattered dreams? What about these?

Can these be lifted at the cross as well?

What happened at the cross

The scene of Christ's crucifixion was far more than a brutal execution. It was a display of power greater than human eyes could see. Colossians 2 describes in triumphant detail what happened in the spiritual realm when Jesus hung on the cross.

> *And you, being dead in your sins and the uncircumcision of your flesh, hath he quickened together with him, having forgiven you all trespasses; Blotting out the handwriting of ordinances that was against us, which was contrary to us, and took it out of the way, nailing it to his cross; And*

having spoiled principalities and powers, he made
a shew of them openly, triumphing over them in it.
—COLOSSIANS 2:13–15

Have you ever considered that every load in your life is the direct result of sin and Satan? It's not always the direct result of *personal* sin, but without sin, there would be no burdens. Romans 8:22–23 points out that we are not alone in our burdens; even creation itself groans under the weight of sin. "For we know that the whole creation groaneth and travaileth in pain together until now. And not only they, but ourselves also, which have the firstfruits of the Spirit, even we ourselves groan within ourselves, waiting for the adoption, to wit, the redemption of our body."

When Jesus died on the cross, He paid in full for sin—and for the resulting burdens of sin. He bore on Him not only our sin, but our griefs and sorrows as well. "Surely he hath borne our griefs, and carried our sorrows…he was wounded for our transgressions, he was bruised for our iniquities: the chastisement of our peace was upon him; and with his stripes we are healed" (Isaiah 53:4–5).

Although we have been redeemed by Christ, we still live in a fallen world, and we still experience burdens. And yet, we do not carry these burdens on our own shoulders. The glad reality is that Jesus already bore them, and in Him, we can know rest and peace.

Paul said it: "I am crucified with Christ: nevertheless I live; yet not I, but Christ liveth in me" (Galatians 2:20). In Christ, Paul knew that he was dead to sin and free from bearing his own burdens. This comes back to who we are (Paul said "I am"—not "I hope to be"). It's a reality.

The cross is more than a starting place; it is the place where we must live.

The heavy lifting

When you reflect on one word—*grace*—you will realize the full reality of what happened on the cross. In that gruesome scene, the awesome justice and tender grace of God were mutually displayed. In His love, God satisfied His justice through His own Son, and He freely extended His grace.

We know little of God's grace—in our dealings with others and in our relationship with God. And because we don't understand grace, we just keep trying harder.

We try harder to understand the unexplainable.

We try harder to make our lives work out.

We try harder to exceed the expectations of others.

And we push others to try harder too.

In fact, often we're trying so hard to carry our loads and prod others to carry theirs, that when the Burden Bearer, who already bore our load, calls, "Cast your cares on Me; I care for you," we don't even hear Him. Or we don't believe Him.

But, Jesus *has* already borne our load. And when we trust in His grace, we can experience His power. As the missionary Hudson Taylor said, "Many Christians estimate difficulties in light of their own resources, and thus attempt little and often fail in the little they attempt. All God's giants have been weak men who did great things for God because they reckoned on His power and presence with them."

Glory in the cross

Ordinary Lifters take both pleasure and pride in how much they can lift. Like Carrier, they draw their identity from the weight they can carry, and they draw their "village worth" by what weight others see them carry.

But Lifters who know the Burden Bearer and understand the happy realities of His death and resurrection, no longer find pleasure or pride in their loads. Leaving the traditional glories of the Lifters, they glory in the cross of Jesus Christ.

Paul was this type of Lifter, for he said, "God forbid that I should glory, save in the cross of our Lord Jesus Christ, by whom the world is crucified unto me, and I unto the world" (Galatians 6:14).

Do you glory in the cross? Or in your strength to carry heavy loads?

The preacher G. Campbell Morgan told his students, "Inevitably, sooner or later, there comes a crisis...in which we are brought to the appalling sense of our own incompetence and weakness. That is a great hour...." And so it is, that when we finally acknowledge that God didn't create our shoulders to bear the weights created by sin and suffering, we have the glad opportunity to experience His gracious strength. For the Burden Bearer Himself promised, "My grace is sufficient for thee: for my strength is made perfect in weakness" (2 Corinthians 12:9).

Truly, we have nothing to glory of except the cross of Christ and the grace that has placed us "in Christ."

It is finished

Are you carrying a heavy load? Stand next to Carrier for a moment—linger at the cross. Listen to Jesus declare, "It is finished!" And watch Him prove it by rising from the dead three days later. Think of His love for you—His powerful, tender love. And leave your burden there—at the cross.

CHAPTER SIX

A Better Way

"ON OUR WAY to the Cross, you were hoping I was going to give you a heavy load, weren't you, Carrier?"

Carrier blushed at the Burden Bearer's question. "Well, yes," he admitted. "I did so want to carry something for You. I want to still be in Your service."

"And I want you to be as well."

"But I don't even have a Pack anymore. How can I carry anything for You?"

"Actually, Carrier, I *do* want to give you a heavy load—a load so heavy that it weighs *My* heart."

Carrier stood speechless in surprise.

"The load I want to give you is far too heavy for your Pack or for the Pack any Lifter has ever been able to construct. And so, I have a better way for you to carry it."

Carrier didn't know where to begin asking questions. It had never occurred to him to carry a load in anything *but* a Pack. So when the Burden Bearer turned and began walking, Carrier followed speechless.

They walked together for some time, until they reached the top of a mountain that overlooked the old city of Jerusalem. Carrier had a strange sensation that as they hiked they had walked back some thousands of years in time.

"See down there, Carrier?" The Burden Bearer pointed to the city below.

Carrier looked at the crowded streets. Hawkers called out their goods, attempting to lift their voices above the city's noise. Long-bearded Pharisees lifted their robes to keep them clear of the rubble on the street as they silently threaded their way through the crowds. Children playing in and around the streets dodged the donkey carts as they stubbornly defied the dense crowds and pushed toward their destinations. "Umm...it, it sure looked different back then." Carrier wasn't exactly sure what the Burden Bearer was pointing out.

"No, it's exactly the same as today," the Burden Bearer responded.

Carrier saw tears glistening in the Burden Bearer's eyes.

And then, as if it were wrung from His very heart, the Burden Bearer cried out, "O Jerusalem, Jerusalem, which killest the prophets, and stonest them that are sent unto thee; how often would I have gathered thy children together, as a hen doth gather her brood under her wings, and ye would not!" (Luke 13:34).

Carrier looked down at the city again. The scene hadn't changed at all, but it was now different in Carrier's eyes. The streets were no longer full of crowds—they were full of real *people*. The crowd now had faces—men women, boys, and girls who did not know the Burden Bearer; every one of them carrying burdens never meant for humans to shoulder. Carrier thought perhaps he was beginning to understand the burden that pressed on the heart of the Burden Bearer.

"It's a large burden, is it not, Carrier?"

"It's too large for me," Carrier answered simply.

"And too large for the Pack you gave Me." And with that, the Burden Bearer lifted a large wooden beam that was lying near his feet. Carrier had not noticed the beam before, but now he looked at it intently.

It was a long, smooth beam that featured a large curve down and back up at both ends. On either side of each curve, there were large holes bored through the beam, and in the holes had been fitted two wooden bows. In the center of the beam was a swivel to which a pole or chain could be attached.

"It's a yoke!" Carrier exclaimed as he vaguely recognized the unfamiliar object. He looked again to the city below and confirmed his supposition. Sure enough, down below he could see teams of oxen and donkeys pulling their large loads at the outskirts of the city. Across their shoulders were yokes, leveraging the weight behind them.

The Burden Bearer smiled at Carrier's enthusiastic discovery. And then His face grew sober as He began to explain. "I never intended for any Lifter to go through life with a Pack strapped to his back. In fact, I created a world where there would be no burdens at all. But as you know, sin changed that, and there are burdens—burdens too heavy for any Lifter to carry at all, let alone to carry in bulging Packs strapped to their weak shoulders."

Carrier grimaced at the mention of weak shoulders, but he knew it was true. As brave and strong as Lifters tried to be, in the end, they were all very, very weak—especially when their strength was compared to that of the Burden Bearer's.

"I have a better way. A different way." And the Burden Bearer ran his hand along the smooth wood of the yoke. "Come unto me, all ye that labour and are heavy laden, and I will give you rest. Take my yoke upon you, and learn of me; for I am meek and lowly in heart: and ye shall find rest unto your souls. For my yoke is easy, and my burden is light" (Matthew 11:28–30).

Well, of course! Carrier thought. *A yoke is so much better than a Pack. Why would we Lifters exhaust all our strength hoisting Packs when we could ergonomically leverage our strength by pulling with a yoke instead?*

The Burden Bearer seemed to read Carrier's thoughts. "It's not just a better method, Carrier; I'm inviting you to be My partner."

How could an offer so gracious be denied? "Thank You," Carrier said simply.

"Carrier," the Burden Bearer said as He lifted the yoke for His new partner, "I will bear every load that enters your life. It doesn't matter how the burden came to you—who sent it or how heavy it is. But when you share the yoke with Me, you also choose to share the burden of My heart—the care for lost souls who struggle through life without a Burden Bearer."

"It's my pleasure," responded the eager Lifter who had always wanted to carry a heavy load for the Burden Bearer.

And that is how Carrier, the Lifter who entered the world weak and scrawny, who strengthened himself by trying harder, who emptied his Pack and then disposed of it—that is how this very Carrier assumed the place for which he had been created.

In our day of idolized productivity, we measure success by quantifiable results. We create databases and programs that keep track of statistics and compare numerical progress.

We chart productivity and ignore relationships.

We measure time and forget people.

We track statistics and overlook hearts.

And in so doing, we reduce ourselves to live as if we were highly-specialized machines.

Meanwhile, our burdens grow heavier.

And heavier.

But we have no time to deal with the increased weight. After all, emotional and relational loads are not measurable or visible. So they don't count, right?

Often, our own loads are so heavy that we don't have the emotional capacity to notice the burdens those around us are likewise carrying. And so they trudge forward without our help. Or they drop under the load. But we don't notice until they've been out of commission for quite some time—for too long.

When we adopt the mindset that our success in life is determined by the visible and measurable results, we reduce ourselves to human *doings* instead of human *beings*. And we miss the greatest work in life—sharing the burdens Christ calls us to bear.

In inviting us to take His yoke, Christ revealed several truths about burdens, success, and the labor He values most.

Unseen realities

Carrier's Pack may be allegorical, but it's not fictitious. Everybody I know has burdens. You do. I do. Your family does. My family does. Everybody does.

Some of our burdens are known, and some are private. Even the ones that are known are often forgotten by others. They are real, but for all practical purposes invisible.

Human burdens are not invisible to Jesus, however. It is because He sees our loads that He calls, "Come unto me, all ye that labour and are heavy laden" (Matthew 11:28).

But just as real as our burdens is God's strength delivered to us through His grace. When He promised, "My grace is sufficient for thee: for my strength is made perfect in weakness" (2 Corinthians 12:9), He meant every word of it.

The difficulty, then, is not our *burdens;* it is that we do not accept God's offered strength. We insist on carrying our loads squarely on our shoulders when all the while Christ offers to bear our loads if we will share His yoke.

But like Carrier, we are reluctant to release our Packs—our methods for managing and containing the unseen burdens we bear. Yet Christ has a better method—a yoke.

What does the yoke mean? And what are its superior features?

Less strain, more weight

My granddaughter, Delanie, loves the small wagon Terrie and I purchased for her. She loves to pile her wagon with toys, books, trinkets, and any other treasures she can find and pull around the yard. Less than two years old, Delanie isn't nearly strong enough to carry the weight of the entire load from her wagon in her arms. But she can easily pull it in the wagon.

When Christ allows burdens in our lives, He doesn't intend for us to carry them in our arms or on our backs. When our burdens are carried in these positions, we will eventually be crushed. And this is why when Jesus called us to learn of Him, He didn't offer to strap another Pack on our backs. Instead, He invited us to share His yoke.

Not only is pulling a better method than lifting, but a yoke provides the benefit of sharing the load rather than pulling it alone.

Those who still today work with yoked oxen know that a team of oxen can pull more than double the combined weight that two single oxen could pull. These powerful animals extend their strength through synergy.

And in our case, the synergy that Christ offers is not just double what you and I could pull. It is the opportunity to connect our weakness to His strength. The reason His yoke is easy and His burden light is because *He* carries the burden.

Welcome, Pardner!

Perhaps the heaviest burden Christians carry is loneliness. When we are sure of sympathy and supported by encouragement, we can go further, longer, and faster. Alone, however, we become disheartened and desolate.

But a yoke signifies unity. To accept Christ's offer to take His yoke means that we will never carry our burdens alone again. The Burden Bearer whom we serve never leaves His own.

It's incredible, really, that God would invite us to share His yoke. And He does it on such gracious terms—He calls us His *friends*.

> *Henceforth I call you not servants; for the servant knoweth not what his lord doeth: but I have called you friends; for all things that I have heard of my Father I have made known unto you. Ye have not chosen me, but I have chosen you, and ordained you, that ye should go and bring forth fruit, and that your fruit should remain: that whatsoever ye shall ask of the Father in my name, he may give it you.*
> —JOHN 15:15–16

Remember the old Wild West shows in which a broke outlaw would find a wealthy greenhorn and offer to accept the naive greenhorn in as a partner? The benefits of those deals were one-sided. The outlaw's intentions were not to *help* the greenhorn, but to *use* him. To keep the long end of the stick, the outlaw made sure he held the advantage in knowledge, skill, connections... and ammunition.

When Jesus offers His yoke, He doesn't *use* us; He *fulfills* us. It's a partnership in which He makes us His friends—His equals in the work. What grace! What an offer!

As Jesus' partner in the yoke, we no longer carry the responsibility of the outcome. We simply share in the yoke and in the rewards.

One word of caution is important in this partnership, however. We must remember Whose yoke we are in. Sometimes we get mixed up and think that Christ is pulling *our* yoke, instead of the other way around. We expect Him to fulfill *our* agenda and to operate on *our* timetable. In a strange turning of our minds, we actually try to *use* Him when He so graciously invited us. If you believe that you are in Christ's yoke, but you find yourself frustrated and agitated, consider if you have the roles reversed.

Christ offers to make each of us His partner, and He retains the ownership of the burden. Sometimes we are eager to do *for* Christ what in reality He wants to do *through* us.

Room to grow

Have you ever asked someone to help you and then become so frustrated with their inept abilities that you eventually urged them to leave?

When my boys were small, I remember their eagerness to help me with any kind of hands-on project. Although they were clumsy and awkward at handling the tools and following the steps, I enjoyed working with them, and I especially enjoyed teaching them the skills that I knew they would need later.

Included in Jesus' invitation to share His yoke is the call to learn from Him. Not only does He offer to teach us how to pull properly, but He recognizes that we don't have it all together before we start. He gives us room to grow.

Jesus' methods in the yoke are not only different from ours, but they are the exact opposite of ours. Our way is much like Carrier's. We value strength and want to appear strong at all costs. Our way is the "I can do it all by myself" way of my three-year-old grandson. As slow as we are to recognize it and as much as we hate to admit it, our way is proud and haughty. We want to be noticed for our strengths and valued for our skills.

Jesus' way is paradoxically reversed. He invites, "learn of me; for I am meek and lowly in heart: and ye shall find rest unto your souls." Our way is exhausting; Jesus' way is refreshing. Our way is weakening; Jesus' way is strengthening. Proverbs 10:29 promises, "The way of the LORD is strength to the upright."

When we insist on carrying burdens our way, we actually repel God. But when we humbly give our burdens to Him and submit to pull with meek humility in His yoke, we link with His grace. Perhaps this is why the admonition to humble ourselves and the promise that Christ will carry our burdens is in the same passage: "God resisteth the proud, and giveth grace to the humble. Humble yourselves therefore under the mighty hand of God, that he may exalt you in due time: Casting all your care upon him; for he careth for you" (1 Peter 5:5–7).

Unexpected adjectives

What words would you use to describe manual labor, such as would be performed in a yoke? Miserable? Difficult? Heavy? Toilsome? Dreaded?

Jesus used surprising adjectives to describe His yoke: "For my yoke is easy, and my burden is light."

These are not "happy talk" words. They are to be the reality for the child of God who is leaving the burden with Christ while committing to serve alongside Him.

One Christian wrote to his family, "Jesus is precious. His service is perfect freedom. His yoke is easy and His burden light. Joy and peace His people have indeed." What sort of person would you expect penned these words? A successful businessman? A young, newly-married husband? Or maybe a seasoned pastor?

Actually, the writer was a twenty-one-year-old single missionary en route to China—the country in whose spiritual service he would eventually bury seven children and two wives, the country where he would eventually assume the responsibility of 850 fellow missionaries and 205 mission stations.

And yet, far from burdened, Hudson Taylor maintained to the end of his life the joy and freedom of spirit that come when sharing Christ's easy yoke and light burden. The title of his favorite hymn reflected the peace of his soul: "Jesus, I Am Resting, Resting."

When we shed our Packs and choose Jesus' yoke, we change the adjectives used to describe our work. Whereas we were harried and flustered or burdened and drained, we are now joyous and free. His yoke *is* easy, and His burden *is* light.

The burden of His heart

Before we conclude this chapter, take a moment to consider what the burden of Jesus' heart actually is. What is this burden that He asks us to share?

It is the only burden that was not lifted at the cross—the burden for souls.

Would you make this burden yours? You can't bear it on your back or in any of the positions we try to bear burdens in our own strength. You can only bear it in the yoke with Christ.

Do you want to carry a heavy load for your Burden Bearer? Then share in His burden for the eternal souls of others. "For the love of Christ constraineth us; because we thus judge, that if one died for all, then were all dead: And that he died for all, that they which live should not henceforth live unto themselves, but unto him which died for them, and rose again" (2 Corinthians 5:14–15).

Oh, Lifter, live for and serve with the Burden Bearer!

CONCLUSION TO PART 2

WE COULD SPEND a lifetime filling, refilling, and emptying our Packs. And frankly, that is what most of us do.

But the alternative is far better—to spend a lifetime united with Christ in His yoke.

Our natural tendency is to be consumed with our burdens. Even in the process of handing them over to Christ we tend to focus on our pain. But once we exchange our Pack for Christ's yoke, our focus redirects. In the yoke with the Burden Bearer, we have the amazing opportunity to, with Him, lift the burdens of others.

As we conclude part two of this book, we round a corner. Since we have taken on Christ's yoke, we will now look specifically at the unique challenges and burdens that we encounter through serving in the yoke with Christ. In the chapters ahead, we unearth the significance of grace and rest, the pain of ministry, the sovereignty of God, and the incredible rewards for our labor.

Before you read further, I encourage you to spend a moment to commit, or to recommit, to take Christ's yoke upon you and learn of Him. His yoke is easy and His burden is light.

Personal Reflections

_____

_____

_____

_____

_____

_____

_____

_____

_____

_____

_____

_____

_____

_____

_____

_____

_____

_____

PART THREE

Serving in Christ's Yoke

Bear ye one another's burdens, and so fulfil the law
of Christ.—GALATIANS 6:2

Not that we are sufficient of ourselves to think any thing as of
ourselves; but our sufficiency is of God; Who also hath made us
able ministers…—2 CORINTHIANS 3:5–6

For which cause we faint not; but though our outward man
perish, yet the inward man is renewed day by day. For our
light affliction, which is but for a moment, worketh for us a far
more exceeding and eternal weight of glory; While we look not
at the things which are seen, but at the things which are not
seen: for the things which are seen are temporal; but the things
which are not seen are eternal.—2 CORINTHIANS 4:16–18

CHAPTER SEVEN

Learning to Rest

CARRIER EASILY SETTLED into the new routines of yoke-bearing. In fact, he didn't just settle in—he *loved* it. *I was made for this,* he frequently thought. *Yoke-bearing may be work, but it's a work I want to be engaged in for the rest of my life.*

Carrier delighted in every mile traveled with the Burden Bearer and was always up early, eager and ready to begin the day's labor. Sometimes he even felt he was more enthusiastic to move forward than the Burden Bearer Himself. All too often for Carrier's comfort, the Burden Bearer paused. These forced rests prohibited Carrier from dragging the yoke further, and when he turned his dismayed face toward the Burden Bearer, he was met with the gentle reminder, "Follow Me; don't rush ahead." Sometimes the Burden Bearer would even insist that they rest at the side of the road. During these periods, Carrier was beside himself with mounting impatience.

During one of these rests, a light-footed runner hailed them. "Why are you stopped?" he asked incredulously.

Carrier immediately recognized their common thirst for speed but since he was loyal to the Burden Bearer, he replied matter-of-factly, "We needed to rest." (It would have been more accurate to say, "*I* needed to rest, and the Burden Bearer knew it and made me." But Carrier wasn't ready to be *that* transparent.)

"Rest?" the runner scoffed. "Who needs rest?" And then, with a significant look at the yoke, he reconsidered. "Ah, well, rest if you need to; I'm off. Good to meet you."

"Wait, we *didn't* meet," Carrier reminded him. "I'm Carrier."

"Yes, I see; and I'm Sprinter. See you later." And with that, he was gone.

Carrier's sigh as his gaze followed Sprinter's swift departure spoke the longing in his heart. The Burden Bearer read Carrier's disappointment: "I know, Carrier. You wish you could travel that fast, too."

"It's not that…well, it's…yes, see, I…" but no matter how Carrier broached his explanation, he couldn't find a way around insinuating that he doubted the Burden Bearer's wisdom in rest or speed of travel.

The Burden Bearer took to the road again, and both were silent for several minutes.

"Being in My yoke, Carrier," the Burden Bearer finally began, "means that you must travel at My speed."

Carrier nodded. He knew—he had noticed from almost the very beginning of his journey in the Burden Bearer's yoke.

"But that's not all. It also means that we travel with a purpose. Yes, we often find ourselves traveling more slowly than a runner ever would—because we are accomplishing something."

Carrier hadn't considered this before, and he turned the thought over in his mind several times before responding. "So Sprinter—he didn't have a yoke, he ran alone—he's not serving You?"

"He started out in My yoke," the Burden Bearer responded sorrowfully, "but he couldn't take the pace. So he discarded the yoke and took off."

"So he isn't helping You at all anymore?" Carrier was now incredulous.

The Burden Bearer smiled and answered Carrier's question with a question of His own. "Were you serving Me before you gave me your Pack and took My yoke?"

"Yes, but not with nearly the efficiency or the…."

"Fruitfulness?"

"Yes, fruitfulness. I was helping, but it was in my strength; and my strength can only go so far."

"Exactly. Sprinter's heart is to serve Me, and he's straining every muscle in his body to run for Me. And it seems to you he is accomplishing much more than you, in a fraction of the time, doesn't it?"

Carrier nodded.

"But, Carrier, our journey is a marathon, not a sprint. You can drop this yoke and sprint forward, but you'll wear out. The nature of our journey requires that you run with patience—with endurance—the race that is set before *you*."

Carrier nodded in understanding.

"And one more thing, Carrier, let Me set the speed. I really do know when you need rest and how to replenish you for the journey."

Several years ago, after preaching in a foreign country, a ministry friend took my wife and me to a remote hotel "resort" in Central America for a night and day of rest before our return flight home. After an eventful, frightful journey on deteriorating roads, we arrived for our day of "rest."

No one behind the desk of this resort, which was located in a particularly humid jungle region, spoke English. They were able to make us understand, however, that there was no record of our reservation, and for a while it looked like there was no room for the night.

We finally obtained a key and headed to our room, only to discover that, in addition to the lack of air conditioning, it contained the most unusual beds we had ever seen. The two single beds had mattresses crafted from barn hay cased in a heavy cloth. The hay poked through the fabric of the mattresses, through the sheets of the bed, and through the skin of the occupants. Additionally, our beds were approximately five and a half feet long—definitely inadequate space for my 6' 2" frame.

We emerged from our "restful" night bearing in our bodies the "marks of the mattress" and ready to head home for real rest!

Restless

Most of us live without truly enjoying spiritual, emotional, and sometimes even physical rest. Our culture and our own bent toward drivenness contrive together to keep us from rest.

In stark contrast to our restless living, Jesus extends His gracious offer:

> *Come unto me, all ye that labour and are heavy laden, and I will give you rest. Take my yoke upon you, and learn of me; for I am meek and lowly in heart: and ye shall find rest unto your souls. For my yoke is easy, and my burden is light.*
> —MATTHEW 11:28–30

Most of us who have served the Lord any length of time can quote these verses, but how often do we really take Christ up on His offer? We complain of fatigue, burnout, overload, and exhaustion, but do we accept Christ's invitation to rest?

If we are to effectively serve in Christ's yoke, we absolutely must learn to rest.

Beside still waters

Throughout the Gospels, we see Jesus seeking out rest through solitude: "And in the morning, rising up a great while before day, he went out, and departed into a solitary place, and there prayed" (Mark 1:35). We also see Him teaching His disciples the importance of rest: "And he said unto them, Come ye yourselves apart into a desert place, and rest a while: for there were many coming and going, and they had no leisure so much as to eat" (Mark 6:31).

I believe we can accurately say that true rest is a divine activity. God made the seventh day to be holy as a day of rest.

For many years, I neglected this Christlike pattern. Even today it is easy to get caught in the adrenaline rush of excitement and urgency, and I fail to take time for rest. That very adrenaline addiction can be so overpowering that we follow it into a life pattern that is destructive to health, relationships, and long-term planning. Additionally, the strong and influential rhythms of our culture can generate a faux sense of guilt when we contemplate availing ourselves to those needed seasons alone with Jesus in the desert.

We Americans have turned the principles of rest inside out and backward. Think of it—we often need time to recoup from our *vacations*. We have spent time, energy, and money on mere temporal busyness. And while there may be temporary relief in such outings, the rest of which Jesus spoke is much deeper than can be provided by a quick trip out of town. A true understanding of rest is found, in fact, when activity ceases. When was the last time you took time to just "Be still, and know that I am God" (Psalm 46:10)? It is in that stillness—in the atmosphere of silence—we find our sensitivity to God increased and our self-created anxiety decreased.

If you are an organizer or a "Type A" person, you will be tempted to feel you are losing control of needed project management, and you will find very "spiritual" reasons to resist rest. The problem is that the illusion of control will only develop more anxiety in your life.

The truth is, God is in control. Jesus is Lord. It is good for us that He is in control, and it is good to put our heads down to rest and let God take care of His own universe.

While we are busy trying to be all we can be, the Holy Spirit is offering to be what we truly need. He longs to lead us to still waters and nourishing pastures where we will find rest for our souls. While our continual restlessness and built-up anxiety prevent His strength and creativity from guiding us, He invites us to a life of rest in Him.

There is no doubt that we need times to pull away for physical refreshment. But Jesus promises His rest even when we are in the midst of our routines of service. We need to learn not only how to find rest for our bodies, but for our souls as well.

Come unto Me

In one word—*come*—Jesus invites us to abandon the rat race and experience real rest. In vivid contrast to our frenzied lives, rest is a common theme throughout Scripture:

> *Rest in the* LORD, *and wait patiently for him…*
> —PSALM 37:7

> *Be still, and know that I am God: I will be exalted among the heathen, I will be exalted in the earth.*
> —PSALM 46:10

> *Return unto thy rest, O my soul; for the* LORD *hath
> dealt bountifully with thee.*—PSALM 116:7

Christ's offer to rest begins with an invitation to Himself. "Come unto Me." The deepest, most satisfying rest we will ever find is in Christ Himself.

In fact, true rest doesn't begin until we receive Christ as our Saviour. At that point, we enter into His eternal rest. And that is only the beginning. As we come to the Lord and join His yoke, we find continued rest by leaning on Christ and trusting in Him as we serve.

Soul-rest then, is primarily about knowing Jesus. It is amazing that in ministry, without ever intending for it to happen, our interest shifts from loving God supremely to loving what we do for God. In the hurried pace and appearance-driven mindset of our culture, we become so wrapped up in our actions and productivity that we neglect our relationship with Jesus.

The greatest challenge, as well as the greatest need, for those of us who have committed to serve in Christ's yoke is to keep our love for Jesus flourishing. The purpose of the Christian life is to know Him (Philippians 3:10). It's not primarily about what we do for God, but about who we are before Him—and especially, about who He is.

Do you know Him well? Do you take time to fellowship with Him? Do you purposefully pull yourself from the current to daily spend time in fellowship with the Lord through His Word? Only in the pursuit of Christ can we find real rest.

If the yoke is easy, why am I exhausted?

Perhaps, like me, you find yourself fatigued by the unending demands of life and service. Sometimes we're tempted to think that the way to find rest is to run from it all—to bolt.

But quitting is the worst way to rest. The rest Christ offers is not the *absence* of a yoke; rather it is the acceptance of the *right* yoke. We find rest by serving in His easy yoke.

Yes, we all reach points of fatigue and need rest. But if we are continually exhausted, it's not a result of Jesus' yoke. It may be that we are serving in the power of the flesh—that we are bearing the burden of ministry in the old ways of the Lifters—rather than allowing Christ to bear our load. It may be that we are serving for the approval of people rather than for the Lord alone. Or, it may be that we are actually straining to pull more than our own yoke. Sometimes we simply need to ask the Lord for wisdom in where we invest our time and energy.

The divine cooperative

Our natural tendency is to attempt to carry the load ourselves. The very nature of our self-attempts places us in the position of rejecting Jesus' invitation. While He said, "learn of me; for I am meek and lowly in heart," we ignore the need for meekness and humility, proudly attempting to pull our load in the power of the flesh. We may feel successful for awhile, but eventually we find ourselves exhausted, discouraged, and burnt out.

In Bible times, there were two kinds of yokes used for animals. The first kind was designed to divide the load so that the two animals yoked together would equally share the weight. The second kind of yoke was a training yoke, designed so a younger, less-experienced animal would learn the unity of a yoke while the trained animal actually pulled the weight of the burden.

It is this second yoke that Jesus offers us. He carries the load and burden; we learn to walk in unity with Him.

The hardest taskmasters

Sometimes we neglect Christ's yoke altogether and instead assume a hard yoke—a yoke of other people's making. Rather than offering all of our service "as to the Lord" (Colossians 3:23), we serve to meet the approval and gain the acceptance of others.

I've found myself in this yoke more than I'd like to admit— often even without realizing it. There's just something inside of us that wants approval for what we do. And forgetting to look to the Lord to meet this need for affirmation, we are prone to look to others. This is a dangerous yoke to serve in, for we soon learn what difficult taskmasters we have brought ourselves under. People are fickle. People are demanding. People are unpredictable. People have shifting expectations.

Serving for the approval of people is always a losing—and exhausting—proposition. When we serve for others' acceptance, we find ourselves overloaded, resentful, and disillusioned. But when we pour our energy into serving the Lord, we find that He replenishes and reinvigorates us by His grace.

Strength through knowledge

God also provides strength to serve Him through a knowledge of Him. Second Peter 3:18 even links grace and knowledge together: "But grow in grace, and in the knowledge of our Lord and Saviour Jesus Christ."

We weary ourselves of service when we attempt to serve without knowledge. Learning to rest, in fact, includes a determination to grow in our knowledge of Christ. As we study God's Word and apply His truths to our own lives, we learn how to more effectively live His principles. And especially, as we study God's Word, we learn more of Jesus Himself.

Our culture today would indicate that amusement is an avenue of rest. Society is saturated with opportunities for amusement. But, while measured amounts of recreation are necessary and beneficial, continual amusement is not really the answer to rest.

The word *muse* means "to think." The prefix *a* is from Latin and means "no." So *amusement* literally means "not to think." Yes, we sometimes do need to give our minds a break, but a life filled with amusement is not the type of rest Jesus offers. (Do we really want to be rested zombies? Or do we want to be renewed yoke bearers?)

When we apply ourselves to growth—to purposefully learning how to wear and best serve in Christ's easy yoke—we gain a level of rest that can only come from the Holy Spirit. We learn, both by study and personal experience, to abide in Christ and rest in Him as we serve.

There is rest in growth. Continue learning. Find rest through instruction from God's Word.

Refreshment

Are you exhausted? Are you needing soul-deep refreshment?

Remember, the answer to fatigue is not quitting; it is learning to rest and learning to bear Christ's easy yoke with His meekness and humility.

Refuse to bolt because you are exhausted. Rather, draw closer to Christ Himself by taking His yoke and centering your service on Him alone. Learn of Him. Study His ways. Take time to drink from the living water He provides through His Word. And rest in His fullness.

CHAPTER EIGHT

The Language of Grace

THE BURDEN BEARER'S yoke was easy, but Carrier soon discovered that it wasn't painless. Blisters began to develop where the yoke rubbed his shoulders, and his feet were becoming raw and painful. He certainly wasn't complaining about taking time to rest now.

Always one to grin and bear it (or grit and persevere), Carrier pressed forward one step at a time.

Finally, Carrier could bear it no longer. Asking to pause, he displayed his wounds, which were by now bleeding sores, to the Burden Bearer. "Why," he queried, "why must I suffer like this? Why must burden bearing include pain?"

The Burden Bearer drew a bottle of salve from His coat. "Let Me treat those wounds, Carrier. I never wanted you to ignore them."

Carrier winced as the Burden Bearer spread the ointment on the tender places, and then he relaxed in relief as the ointment soothed the pain. "Thank you. What's the ointment?"

"It's called Comfort, but its ingredients are My Word and My Spirit."

Carrier watched as the Burden Bearer replaced the top to the bottle. And then, with a stifled gasp he noticed—or rather, he was reminded. As the Burden Bearer turned His hand about the bottle, Carrier saw once again the ugly wounds riven through His palms.

The Burden Bearer read Carrier's thoughts. "I did it gladly—for you."

"Thank You." But somehow the words seemed small, almost trite, in view of those wounds.

Carrier remembered the Cross as the Burden Bearer spoke. "I was wounded for your transgressions and bruised for your iniquities. I suffered so that you could be healed."

Carrier didn't know what to say, so he repeated his former words, "thank You." This time, they sounded even less fitting.

The Burden Bearer stood up. "It did cost Me a great deal, but I did it out of choice—for love. Now you must also sometimes suffer so that you can share the comfort which I have given you." With a smile, He handed Carrier the bottle of ointment.

This time, Carrier said nothing. "Thank You" was too small. It almost seemed more fitting to say, "I'm sorry I even thought to complain." But what Carrier really wished he knew how to put into words was his newly-birthed desire to pass on this Comfort to others. The blistered shoulders and the sore feet paled into insignificance when compared to his receiving the precious ointment.

Before they continued on their way, the Burden Bearer adjusted the yoke so it wouldn't rub Carrier's blisters. "Your feet may grow sore, but the yoke shouldn't be rubbing like that. Let's fix it next time *before* it rubs so deep."

Once again, Carrier thanked the Burden Bearer. Carrier then put the bottle of ointment into his pocket. "For safe keeping," he explained. "I have a feeling there's someone just up ahead who's going to need this."

If you have ever studied a foreign language, you can relate to the exhausting, head-bashing stress of trying to express your ideas through another person's vocabulary, grammar, and cultural thought processes. And if your first language happened to be English, and your hopeful language happened to be Korean, you definitely understand why linguistic analysts have identified Korean as one of the most difficult second languages for an English-speaker to learn.

When my parents moved our family to Seoul, South Korea, I was beginning my first year of high school. Thankfully, I was able to attend an English-speaking school, but I did attempt to learn the Korean language as well.

I never reached a high level of fluency, but I did learn enough to get by on the streets; and I am thankful to retain enough Korean today that I can order in a restaurant or introduce someone to a Gospel tract. Not only does Korean have a completely different alphabet and grammar structure than English, but it has a complicated social register that denotes levels of respect. So when conjugating·

sentences, not only do you consider the person to whom you are speaking, but you also consider your relationship to that person. And should you be relating a story or conversation in third person, you must consider the relationships and social stratification of all those involved. It's a beautifully harrowing language.

There is a language none of us has to learn—it's common to every nationality and group of people, defying cultural variances and grammatical peculiarities. This language—the language of suffering—is universal. Every one of us knows this language, and every one of us has experience in its various levels and intricacies.

Service in Christ's yoke in no way exempts us from suffering. But let's not forget that our fellow yoke-mate fully understands the language of suffering. Hebrews 4:15 tells us, "For we have not an high priest which cannot be touched with the feeling of our infirmities; but was in all points tempted like as we are, yet without sin." At the deepest level, Jesus understands even the unutterable cries of our soul when we are fast in the grip of pain.

And yet, Jesus is multilingual. He not only understands our suffering, but He speaks to us in grace. Even as He hears our pleas of suffering, He knows and makes available to us the limitless supply of God to meet those needs. Hebrews 4:16 urges, "Let us therefore come boldly unto the throne of grace, that we may obtain mercy, and find grace to help in time of need."

This language of grace is more foreign to our human understanding than the language of suffering. And yet, if we are to serve in Christ's yoke, we must learn to both understand and speak this beautiful language of the Burden Bearer.

He understands us, *and* He can help us. Concurrent to comforting us in our suffering, He speaks words of grace to our souls. Through those very words of grace, He teaches *us* to speak the language of grace that we might comfort others.

Rhythms of grace

Comprised of more than sounds, language is replete with rhythms. And those rhythms never seem more significant than when you are listening to a foreign speaker communicating in your language without it! Without proper emphasis and rhythm, language is at best difficult to understand; more often, it is misunderstood.

Of course, the first language of us Lifters is the harsh "try harder" language. But the Burden Bearer's gentle language is that of grace. By grace He saved us (Ephesians 2:8). By grace He conforms us to His likeness (2 Corinthians 3:18). And by grace He upholds and sustains us through the difficult times of life (2 Corinthians 12:9).

As the Burden Bearer teaches us the language of grace, He wants us to learn its rhythms—to make its cadence our own drive. In fact, He desires that we so learn the simple rhythms of this language that it does not remain our "second language"—one to fall back on only when we find we can't try hard enough to meet present demands. He desires that it become our *preferred* language—one that, through the coaching of the Holy Spirit, we express by default.

Present tense

The language of grace knows only the present verb tense.

When Christ offered Paul His sufficient grace, He neither said, "My grace *will be* sufficient for you," nor, "My grace *was* sufficient for you." Rather, He said, "My grace *is* sufficient for you" (2 Corinthians 12:9). That is the language of grace—always in the present tense.

In the late 1800s, a pastor by the name of William Webb-Peploe lost his youngest child. On the Saturday after his little one's funeral, he prepared to preach to his people from 2 Corinthians 12:9 about God's sufficient grace. And yet, even as he prepared the message, he found his own aching heart doubting the truth of this verse. He finally laid down his pen, knelt by his desk, and cried out, "Lord, let Your grace be sufficient for me."

As Pastor Webb-Peploe looked up, his eye caught a framed Scripture verse given to him by his mother a few days previously. It was the very text from which he was preparing to preach. The word "is" in the verse stood out in a bold red, contrasted against the rest of the text: "My grace IS sufficient for thee."

That single word reminded the pastor that God's grace is not something we hope and plead for. It *is* always available, and it *is* always sufficient. Years later he said, "Never turn God's facts into hopes or prayers, but simply use them as realities; and you will find them powerful as you believe them."

Do you need God's grace? It is sufficient. Right now. For you.

Speaking the dialects

If you've studied a foreign language, you can relate to how much easier it is to *understand* it than it is to *speak* it. Listening to foreign sounds is one thing, but trying to frame those sounds with your own mouth and order them to make sense is another thing entirely. At first, the words come out so different sounding than you hear them, and you'd better have a good sense of humor if you intend to make it past the first few attempts!

But learning to speak the language of grace—including its dialects of praise and comfort—is vital if you are to serve in the yoke with the Burden Bearer. In fact, this is the heart of yoke-sharing. It is sharing the burden of God's heart and speaking His words of grace and comfort to those who are hurting.

Sometimes it feels awkward. Sometimes it pulls you far out of your comfort zone. Sometimes it brings added pain into your own life as it calls you to seek out and bind wounded, broken hearts.

But on the other hand, it is a joy. For the language of grace contains the words of life, hope, and healing. As laborers together with God, we have the privilege of directing hurting hearts to the only one who can bear their burdens and heal their wounds.

Yes, it is much easier to *receive* grace and comfort than it is to *give* it. But don't lose heart. As you learn the language of grace, you find it is far more rewarding and fulfilling to serve with the Burden Bearer as an extension of His grace to those around us.

And just as fluency in a foreign language cannot come without taking the effort to speak it, as we speak God's Words of grace, we find that we ourselves learn them more fully.

Fruit of our lips

What does the language of grace sound like when we speak it? Hebrews 13:15 provides the answer, "By him therefore let us offer the sacrifice of praise to God continually, that is, the fruit of our lips giving thanks to his name."

When we offer God the sacrifice of praise even in the midst of hardships, we are choosing to speak the language of grace. Such sacrifices turn our burdens into platforms in which God's grace is displayed.

This was the experience of Paul and Silas when they first entered the city of Philippi. Acts 16 records how they were misunderstood, falsely accused, beaten, and imprisoned. Yet these godly men chose to offer the sacrifice of praise. "And at midnight Paul and Silas prayed, and sang praises unto God: and the prisoners heard them" (Acts 16:25). And what was the result of their praise? The jailer heard the words of grace and was saved that very night.

We may find comfort in meditating on God's sufficient grace; but we find joy, and we minister to others, when we offer the sacrifice of praise with our lips.

A word fitly spoken

If there has ever been a time in my life when I needed a word of encouragement, it was the Sunday morning after our eldest son was diagnosed with cancer. In God's providence, we had scheduled a guest preacher for our church months earlier—long before I had any idea of the trial our family would be facing at that time.

As the guest evangelist preached, the Lord graciously used his message to give me the hope and strength I needed. The message was from Psalm 11:1–3 on "When the Foundations Fall"—what to do when you feel as if your life is crumbling underneath you. Through these three verses, he reminded us—and *me* especially—that regardless of our current circumstances we can still trust God and look through the eyes of faith to the promises of God to work for our good.

The preacher's words on that morning reminded me of Proverbs 25:11, "A word fitly spoken is like apples of gold in pictures of silver" and Proverbs 15:23, "…a word spoken in due season, how good is it!"

Truly, we have no help but the truths of God's Word to offer those who are hurting. Pep talk and positive thinking only provide temporal help at best. But God's Word is a mine of grace and truth. It brings healing and comfort, and it focuses hearts on the eternal work that God accomplishes in our lives through suffering.

I know people who seem to resent hearing Scripture at a time of suffering. Perhaps this is because they sense verses being hurled at them as spiritual hand grenades—sort of with an unstated message of, "I don't really care about your need, but remember this verse; it should help." In reality, God's Word is a balm, and it is the only balm that can thoroughly heal the soul.

As partners with the Burden Bearer, it is our job to speak His words with grace, remembering that we are speaking to needy hearts. Like a nurse binding wounds and promising the hope of healing, we share the comfort of the healing words of God.

Lifting loads

The words we speak and the heart behind them have a tremendous power to lift the burdens of others. Galatians 6:2 instructs us that this is part of our duty in the service of the Burden Bearer: "Bear ye one another's burdens, and so fulfill the law of Christ."

It is the heart of the Burden Bearer to lift loads, and our job is to help those around us release their loads from their backs and entrust them to Christ.

And yet, sometimes we shy from the loads of others. We're afraid that we won't know what to say, that we'll come across wrong, that we'll make ourselves vulnerable, or we may just want to avoid feeling their pain.

Lifting loads is not only our privilege; it is also our responsibility. These are the times when others need us most. "A friend loveth at all times, and a brother is born for adversity" (Proverbs 17:17).

If you desire to serve the Burden Bearer, if you have committed to serve in His easy yoke, I challenge you: seek out and minister to those who are hurting and suffering. As someone once wisely said, "Speak to the broken, and you will always have an audience." Determine to both learn *and* speak the language of grace.

Full circle

If there was one man in the first century who knew pain, it was the Apostle Paul. He suffered deeply in every way as he served the Lord. Physically, he was beaten, imprisoned, shipwrecked, hungry, needy, exhausted, and in constant peril for his life

(2 Corinthians 11:23–27). Emotionally, he faced times of being perplexed, troubled, and cast down (2 Corinthians 4:8–9). Spiritually, he carried the responsibility of the needs of the many churches he had labored to plant (2 Corinthians 11:28).

As Paul wrote to the church at Corinth, he told them, "We were pressed out of measure, above strength, insomuch that we despaired even of life" (2 Corinthians 1:8). And yet, he found two blessings in this suffering—first, that God's comfort was sufficient, and second, that experiencing God's comfort made him better able to give it to others.

> *Blessed be God, even the Father of our Lord Jesus Christ, the Father of mercies, and the God of all comfort; Who comforteth us in all our tribulation, that we may be able to comfort them which are in any trouble, by the comfort wherewith we ourselves are comforted of God. For as the sufferings of Christ abound in us, so our consolation also aboundeth by Christ. And whether we be afflicted, it is for your consolation and salvation, which is effectual in the enduring of the same sufferings which we also suffer: or whether we be comforted, it is for your consolation and salvation.*—2 CORINTHIANS 1:3–6

The great joy of those in the service of the Burden Bearer is to serve alongside Christ, comforting hearts with the consolation of God. So what if we must suffer first? We have the all-sufficient, present-tense grace of God. Our afflictions become altars from which we can offer the sacrifice of praise. And our suffering becomes a vehicle by which we can minister God's grace to others.

We receive comfort that we might give comfort. We learn the language of grace that we might speak the language of grace. We give our burdens to Christ that we might bear the burdens of others, while pointing them to *the* Burden Bearer.

CHAPTER NINE

Leave It to the King

DURING THE EARLY days in the yoke with the Burden Bearer, Carrier had been so thrilled to participate that he hadn't paid much attention to what they were actually *doing*. He enjoyed the company of the Burden Bearer, and Carrier's delight was just to know that he was serving Him.

Before long, however, there was that moment of epiphany: *I'm in a yoke because we're pulling something.* It wasn't that Carrier was slow that it took him so long to notice; it was just that he had been so preoccupied with the joy of the shared yoke that he hadn't taken much notice of what it was attached to.

As he turned to look over his shoulder to see exactly what it was they had been pulling, Carrier couldn't believe his eyes! Lifters seemed to be coming from every corner of the village—a great company of them, marching toward the wagon behind him. As each Lifter passed the wagon pulled by Carrier and the Burden Bearer, they would hoist their burdens and deposit them into the wagon. Big burdens, little burdens, great burdens, awkward burdens. In every shape and size they just kept coming. Weighty questions, heavy doubts, hurting hearts. They piled higher and higher. Carrier felt a surge of frustration.

Surely the Burden Bearer could see the problem—they were carrying what seemed like *everyone's* burdens. No wonder it had been so slow going.

"Burden Bearer, we could go so much faster, and our progress would be so much easier, if people would just stop giving me their burdens. What am I to do with them anyway?"

"Pull them in the yoke with Me, of course. This is the purpose of My yoke."

Before Carrier could respond, the road took a hairpin curve and revealed a desert wasteland. "We made a wrong turn?" he asked hopefully.

"Not at all; this is the way." The Burden Bearer's voice was drowned by the howling wind that was stirring up a sandstorm.

Carrier squinted ahead. A few feet in front of them, the path dropped into the sandy dunes. "There *is* no path ahead," he shouted.

The Burden Bearer smiled, but Carrier couldn't see it for the sand that enveloped them. Carrier had never really doubted the Burden Bearer before—not really. But now he hesitated. With a wagon full of other people's burdens behind him and a path of... of nothing in front of him, he wasn't so sure they should plunge forward. It just didn't feel right.

The wind stung Carrier's eyes as he turned to look at the Burden Bearer, hoping to read His expression. But the blowing sand was too thick; he couldn't see anything. Fear reached to grip his heart as he stood in that moment of decision. What if this *was* the wrong way? What if they *didn't* find the path through the desert? If he could just see the Burden Bearer. He tried again, but the sand blinded him.

"Listen to Me, Carrier," the Burden Bearer spoke in a low and gentle voice that penetrated the wind better than Carrier's shouting had done. "To be in the yoke with Me requires surrender to My path. I know where we're going."

"Path?" Carrier was almost delirious with fear now. "There *is* no path." And yet, somehow, having heard the Burden Bearer's voice—even if he couldn't see Him—settled Carrier and steadied his thinking. "I mean, I don't see a path. It looks as though we're headed to nowhere with everybody else's unanswered questions on board behind us."

Again the Burden Bearer smiled, even though—and perhaps because—Carrier couldn't see Him. "Carrier, believe Me. I know the way. I am not counting your steps, but your surrender. Not how fast, but how faithful. Not your tasks, but your trust."

So Carrier trusted—one step at a time. And all during their trek through that miserable desert, Carrier learned to listen to and lean on the words of the Burden Bearer—even though he couldn't see Him.

And to Carrier's joy and surprise, as they journeyed, he found that the desert was studded with oases—paradises of refreshment. Grace, Strength, Restoration, Certain Promises—they each had a name. But they all had one thing in common—an incredible sense of unity with the Burden Bearer.

At each oasis, the Burden Bearer wiped the sand and grit out of Carrier's eyes. Carrier would look around and see that they were still in a desert. The sand was still hot, the wind was still blowing, and the path was still obscured. But then he would look at the Burden Bearer, and he would remember why he was there in the desert. The One whom he trusted more than anyone in the world had led him there.

These oasis moments with the Burden Bearer became treasures to Carrier. In fact, by the time he and the Burden Bearer left the last oasis (which Carrier didn't know was their final stop in the desert), Carrier had decided that the entire desert—discomfort and all—was worth just one of those oases.

September 1, 1939. London, England. Drizzling rain. Tearful goodbyes. Fearful hearts. Operation Pied Piper was under way.

In just three days, London would transport 3.9 million children out of the city to protect them from the massive aerial assault of the German Luftwaffe air force. Wealthier parents had been able to arrange specific destinations for their children—perhaps with relatives or acquaintances in other cities. But most of these children were going to unknown homes and unknown destinations.

The story is told of one young boy who stood on the train platform squinting his eyes into the drizzling rain. A passerby ventured to ask, "Do you know where you are going?"

"No," the boy replied, as the train whistle sounded through the fog, "but the king does."

On our good days, we would make an analogy from that young boy's statement to the sovereign wisdom of *the* King—our Heavenly Father. We would say, *It doesn't matter where I'm going; I trust that my King knows, and that is enough.*

But when we really *don't* know where we're going, when our pain is intense and our path is obscure, when it seems that if we're moving at all we're wandering in circles—on *those* days, we're not always so sure that the King knows.

Does He really know?

Does He really care?

Is He really planning to intervene?

When life is spinning wildly out of control, we wonder. How do we cast a burden on One whose presence or power we question? How can we serve in the yoke of One who seems indifferent to our pain?

A question from the dungeon

Yoke bearing does not insulate us from the pain of suffering. In fact, some of God's greatest servants have known some of the deepest levels of pain. And some of them have asked the most penetrating questions of the King.

Take John the Baptist, for instance.

John was not only Jesus' cousin, but he was also the prophesied forerunner of Christ. His very purpose was to prepare the hearts of Israel for their Messiah. He preached powerful messages on repentance, and he pointed people to their Saviour.

But when John told it like it was to King Herod, the king didn't care to hear that it was wrong to marry his sister-in-law. To silence John's voice, he locked John in the dungeon (Matthew 14:3–4).

There in prison, John faltered. The great proclaimer of truth doubted.

It wasn't the harsh conditions of prison life that wore him down. John had been raised in the desert. He was unconventional and pretty much unmoveable. You can guess that a prison cell wasn't about to make John take back the words which he knew to be true. The dungeon didn't bother John nearly as much as the doubts.

It wasn't that his pride was cut at having his ministry end in a prison. John must have been the most humble servant of Christ. His greatest joy had been for Christ to be magnified—even at John's expense (John 3:30).

What caused the doubt?

We find the answer in the question John sent to Jesus: "Art thou he that should come, or do we look for another?" (Matthew 11:3).

John heard of the works of Jesus. He knew Jesus had the power to perform miracles. And yet, Jesus never came to release him from prison.

It's one thing to say Jesus is the Messiah when He performs miracles for others. It's another thing to believe it when He hasn't released you from unjust imprisonment...while you were promoting His ministry.

It's one thing to say God is sovereign when His blessings fall at your feet. It's another thing to say God is sovereign when your heart is broken and your life is shattered...while you were in His service.

Interestingly, Jesus didn't rebuke John for His question. Yes, it was framed with doubt, but all the same, it was brought to Jesus.

And just as interestingly, Jesus didn't tell John anything he didn't already know. "Jesus answered and said unto them, Go and shew John again those things which ye do hear and see: The blind receive their sight, and the lame walk, the lepers are cleansed, and the deaf hear, the dead are raised up, and the poor have the gospel preached to them" (Matthew 11:4–5). Jesus quoted here from Isaiah 35:5–6, a passage with which John was surely familiar. A passage that prophesied of the Messiah.

John had already known that Jesus performed these miracles, but Jesus helped him put it into perspective. He reminded John that although he wasn't being released from prison, prophecy was being fulfilled. God was in control. God had a larger purpose in mind and a longer perspective in view than the immediate circumstances.

And then Jesus offered a word of encouragement: "And blessed is he, whosoever shall not be offended in me" (Matthew 11:6).

And that was enough for John. His doubts were quieted. His fears were stilled. His heart was settled. The King had spoken.

So, do like John. Bring your questions, your doubts to Jesus. But don't expect a lightning bolt to flash the answer across the sky. Let Him remind you of the truth you already know. Claim His promises. Trust His purposes. We cannot see the sovereignty of God when we are focused on immediate relief.

The Burden Bearer is the King. The King knows where we're going.

A song in the night

In the early 1900s a young evangelist by the name of Luther Bridges accepted an invitation to hold a two-week revival meeting near his wife's parents' home in Kentucky. Leaving his wife and three young sons to enjoy two weeks with family, he traveled on to the meeting.

The Lord blessed the revival services, and at the close of the two weeks, Luther was eager to reunite with his family and share testimonies of God's blessing with his wife. As the final service closed, however, Luther received a long-distance call. He listened in shock as he heard the devastating news: his in-laws' home had been burned to the ground, and his wife and sons had all died in the fire.

Stunned and broken-hearted, Luther couldn't preach any more. Questions turned his mind inside out and incapacitated his ministry. Why would God have done this to him *while he was serving God?*

Gently, the Lord answered His servant—not with reasons (our minds are too limited to fully understand God's reasons), but with His presence. In the pages of God's Word, Luther found both solace and peace. "The LORD is my portion, saith my soul; therefore will I hope in him" (Lamentations 3:24). "He that dwelleth in the secret place of the most High shall abide under the shadow of the Almighty" (Psalm 91:1). With these verses stilling his questions, Luther penned the words to the hymn "He Keeps Me Singing":

There's within my heart a melody,

Jesus whispers sweet and low,

Fear not, I am with thee, peace, be still,

In all of life's ebb and flow.

Jesus, Jesus, Jesus, sweetest Name I know.

Fills my every longing, keeps me singing as I go.

Luther resumed his ministry and served the Lord faithfully until his death, and the King took him Home.

Are you in the dungeon of doubt? Are you in the night of heartache? Are you questioning the care of your Burden Bearer?

He is present. He is in control. He gives songs in the night.

Worse than questions

The Lord is not offended or stumped by our questions. He is not surprised by our doubts. But we hurt ourselves when we refuse to take our questions and doubts to the Burden Bearer.

Questions of suffering are heavy. Continual doubts are crippling. And our coping methods do little to staunch our springs of grief. Left to ourselves, we either drown in our sorrows or drown our sorrows.

Perhaps you've seen someone drown in their sorrows. The load of questions and doubt becomes too weighty to carry, and they simply disappear in their sea of grief. Oh, they may still be physically present, but their spirit is not functioning. Emotionally, relationally, and spiritually, they are far removed from the unbearable reality of the moment.

Then there are those who attempt to drown their sorrows. Alcohol, drugs, food, nicotine, work, even ministry becomes their servant to separate them from the pain. But eventually, these methods become their master as they are addicted to the very things they tried to employ to control their pain.

Scripture provides a better course of action. It's simple, but it's not simplistic.

> *My brethren, count it all joy when ye fall into divers temptations; Knowing this, that the trying of your faith worketh patience. But let patience have her perfect work, that ye may be perfect and entire, wanting nothing. If any of you lack wisdom, let him ask of God, that giveth to all men liberally, and upbraideth not; and it shall be given him. But let him ask in faith, nothing wavering. For he that wavereth is like a wave of the sea driven with the wind and tossed.*—JAMES 1:2–6

Notice two core truths from this passage: Don't be surprised when trials come. Ask God for wisdom in responding to trials.

God may not always show us His purposes in suffering, but He will give us the wisdom to navigate the season of pain if we only ask Him for help. Bring your questions to Him, ask Him for wisdom, and believe that He has a bigger purpose than you can see.

Even as a yoke bearer, *especially* as a yoke bearer, give Him your burdens.

Commit whatever grieves you
Into the gracious hands
Of Him Who never leaves you,
Who Heav'n and earth commands.
Who points the clouds their courses,
Whom winds and waves obey,
He will direct your footsteps
And find for you a way.

On Him place your reliance
If you would be secure;
His work you must consider
If yours is to endure.
According to His counsel
His plan He will pursue;
And what His wisdom chooses
His might will always do.

His hand is never shortened,
All things must serve His might;
His every act is blessing,
His path is purest light.
His work no one can hinder,
His purpose none can stay,
Since He to bless His children
Will always find a way.

Though all the powers of evil
The will of God oppose,
His purpose will not falter,
His pleasure onward goes.
Whatever our God decrees,

Whatever He intends,
Will always be accomplished
By the grace He sends.
—Paul Gerhardt

The spirit of surrender

Committing our burdens, questions, and doubts to God is the opposite of our natural tendency. In his book *The Promise*, Robert Morgan made two statements that have helped give me perspective:

- "Problems dislodge our core of self-sufficient pride and drive us to the Lord."[1]
- "God allows trials in our lives because we have a strong core of inner pride and self sufficiency that works to our long-term detriment."[2]

Often, when I'm questioning God's purposes in the midst of a trial, the Holy Spirit convicts me of the sin of pride. What but pride would make me think I should be given different circumstances?

Jesus Himself surrendered to pain when He knew it was the will of the Father.

> *And he was withdrawn from them about a stone's cast, and kneeled down, and prayed, Saying, Father, if thou be willing, remove this cup from me: nevertheless not my will, but thine, be done. And there appeared an angel unto him from heaven, strengthening him. And being in an agony he*

prayed more earnestly: and his sweat was as it were
great drops of blood falling down to the ground.
—LUKE 22:41–44

Jesus understands suffering. He understands surrender. Will you entrust your questions to Him?

Sometimes it just boils down to surrender—that's what you do before the King.

The sovereignty of God

Although sovereign of the universe, God doesn't remove all pain. But He does bear it for us, and He does promise to make it work for our good.

And we know that all things work together for good
to them that love God, to them who are the called
according to his purpose.—ROMANS 8:28

But the God of all grace, who hath called us unto
his eternal glory by Christ Jesus, after that ye
have suffered a while, make you perfect, stablish,
strengthen, settle you.—1 PETER 5:10

And does God make good on His promises? Ask Abraham. Ask Joseph. Ask David. Ask Rahab. Ask Moses, Esther, Mary, Peter, Paul. Ask *me*! Although I don't yet have an eternal vantage point, and although there are still burdens in my life that I'm waiting to see God work for good, I can look back over the past fifty years and see an incredible track record.

When our son was diagnosed with cancer in 2009, I didn't think I could bear the pain of watching him suffer. And suffer he did. If you've walked the cancer road or have a family member who has, you know the dreadfulness of hospitals, surgeries, blood tests, CAT scans, chemo, sickness, nausea—even now, it is painful to think about. But in that trial, I saw God work in my life in ways so personal and so intricate that I can only credit His sovereignty with the results.

To quote Robert Morgan again, "Somehow, in the wonder-working providence of God, our worst problems become our best pulpits."[3]

Yes, God knows our limits. He carries our burdens. And He redeems our pain.

In the midst of another season of trial in my life, I came across this poem by John Newton, author of the hymn "Amazing Grace." It was helpful to me because it put perspective on how God uses burdens to make us more like Him.

I ASKED THE LORD

I asked the Lord that I might grow
In faith, and love, and every grace;
Might more of His salvation know,
And seek, more earnestly, His face.

'Twas He who taught me thus to pray,
And He, I trust, has answered prayer!
But it has been in such a way
As almost drove me to despair.

I hoped that in some favored hour,
At once He'd answer my request;
And by His love's constraining pow'r
Subdue my sins, and give me rest.

Instead of this, He made me feel
The hidden evils of my heart;
And let the angry pow'rs of Hell
Assault my soul in every part.

Yea more, with His own hand He seemed
Intent to aggravate my woe;
Crossed all the fair designs I schemed,
Blasted my gourds, and laid me low.

Lord why is this, I trembling cried,
Wilt Thou pursue thy worm to death?
"'Tis in this way," the Lord replied,
"I answer prayer for grace and faith.

These inward trials I employ,
From self and pride, to set thee free;
And break thy schemes of earthly joy,
That thou may'st find thy all in Me."

The way through

In pain, we sometimes wonder if our King really knows where we are going. We are tempted to believe that our steps are leading nowhere and our wanderings are pointless. It is then, when we cannot see ahead, that we must say with the psalmist, "When my spirit was overwhelmed within me, then thou knewest my path" (Psalm 142:3).

We are in a yoke with the Burden Bearer, and He doesn't lead to pointless destinations. Besides, the Burden Bearer is our King, and He knows where we are going.

> *When thou passest through the waters, I will be with thee; and through the rivers, they shall not overflow thee: when thou walkest through the fire, thou shalt not be burned; neither shall the flame kindle upon thee.*—ISAIAH 43:2

Give Him your questions. Submit to His direction. He will lead you through.

---

1. Robert Morgan, *The Promise* (B&H Publishing Group, 2010), 165.

2. Ibid.

3. Ibid., 176.

CHAPTER TEN

When Ministry Hurts

"WHAT'S IN YOUR arms, Carrier?" the Burden Bearer asked.

Carrier was happy the Burden Bearer had finally noticed. Since that day when Carrier had first noticed other Lifters dumping their loads into his wagon, he had changed considerably. Back then, he had felt nothing but frustration over others making his load heavier. But *now*, he had actually come to cherish the opportunity to bear others' burdens. It was his favorite aspect of working for the Burden Bearer. He took pleasure in helping to carry the loads, and he especially loved to direct the load-dumpers' attention to the Burden Bearer. He now found himself caring less about the inconveniences or personal sacrifices of yoke-bearing and more about the Lifters who piled their loads into the wagon.

"Oh, it's just several burdens that other Lifters were struggling to hoist into the wagon," he responded. "So I let them hand the loads to me."

"Are they heavy?" This question, as many of the Burden Bearer's questions, was designed to make Carrier think, rather than to inform the Burden Bearer.

"Oh, yes," Carrier beamed. "But I've long since quit caring about pain or difficulty associated with yoke-bearing. It just goes with the territory." Carrier struggled to balance the toppling pile of burdens in his arms.

"But those burdens aren't being pulled by the yoke. They're in your own arms. Why do you say they're associated with yoke-bearing?" the Burden Bearer prodded.

"Well, they're part of what we do together—help people carry their burdens. We do that in our yoke. Since the Lifters couldn't seem to cast them into the wagon, I'm just holding them and tossing them back as I'm able."

"But you're staggering under them!"

It was the word *stagger* that finally arrested Carrier's attention. It reminded him of the old days—the pre-yoke days—when he staggered under the load of his Pack. For the first time since he had begun "helping" Lifters by taking their burdens into his own arms, it occurred to Carrier that maybe there was a better way.

"I called you to share My yoke so you wouldn't have to carry burdens. If you continue pulling a yoke *and* carrying burdens, you'll break down soon."

"I thought I was helping—sacrificing for You." Carrier's voice weakened as his confidence ebbed.

"I'm glad, Carrier, that you've learned to surrender to the pain that comes with yoke-bearing. But when you, on your own, lift burdens that were never meant for a yoke-bearer's shoulders to carry, the pain exceeds your limits. Eventually, the yoke becomes unbearable and unsustainable. Here, why don't you give those loads to Me?"

Carrier dropped them into the Burden Bearer's strong arms, and the Burden Bearer effortlessly tossed the whole pile into the wagon. "There," He smiled, "now you'll be able to stay in My yoke for the long haul. My strength is always sufficient...and your sufficiency is always in My strength."

What happens when twenty-five years of ministry comes crashing down to crush your chest? I thought it was a heart attack, but I learned in the emergency room it was high blood pressure—220/115.

After two similar trips to the emergency room in one week, my doctor ordered a battery of tests and immediate rest. In those weeks of rest, the Holy Spirit gently began to teach me how to share the burden of ministry with Him while still caring for the people who I pastor and love. Especially, He taught me to continue laboring fervently in His yoke while trusting the outcome of the results to Him.

The legitimacy of a pastor's heart

When my family and I moved to Lancaster, California, almost twenty-seven years ago, I was in for a big surprise.

It wasn't the tiny, stuffy, pet-stained duplex we moved into that caught me off guard. Nor was it the duct-taped carpet and weed-covered parking lot of the church building. It wasn't even the fact that there was no salary, and the church owed money to everyone in town and their brother, not to mention to the bank, which was in the process of foreclosing.

The aspect of pastoring that most surprised me was the depth of burdens that I carried for those dozen members. Other than my family, nothing mattered more to me than seeing those under my care grow in spiritual maturity. I prayed for their growth. I fasted for their growth. I studied late into the night for their growth. I loved, served, gave, taught, preached, discipled—poured my life into those people. And it was my greatest joy—and heaviest burden—to see them grow in the Lord.

As a young pastor, I would have been surprised at another aspect of ministry had I possessed the maturity to realize it. You see, I actually believed the ministry would get easier as I got older. Through the years, however, the burdens have *in*creased, not *de*creased. I may not struggle quite as hard through sermon preparation as I did in those early weeks, but God has progressively deepened my love for our church. And in doing so, my burden to see His people grow in Christ has magnified.

The truth is, ministry sometimes hurts.

You may be thinking of the hurt that comes when someone stabs you in the back or slanders your name. And, yes, those are hurts that often come with the territory. When you love someone greatly, you give that person the power to hurt you deeply. But that hurt is secondary to the deeper hurt of which it is only a symptom.

There's another level of hurt. It's the ongoing care you feel for those you are shepherding. Paul likened it to the pain a woman feels as she gives birth (Galatians 4:19). And having served as a pastor now for close to thirty years, I can relate.

I write this chapter as a pastor. This is the sphere of ministry with which God has blessed me. He has entrusted to me the shepherding of a church. But the truths of what to do with the burdens of ministry relate to Christians in any sphere—volunteer or occupational, part time or full time. If you serve in the Burden Bearer's yoke and minister to the needs of people, you will find that ministry sometimes hurts. What do you do with that pain? How do you release those burdens to the Burden Bearer?

Anyone who serves as an undershepherd, be that a pastor, parent, teacher, or another spiritual leader, will carry a burden for his or her flock. Only a hireling can go to bed at night without the care of the flock on his heart.

In Galatians we catch a unique glimpse into the Apostle Paul's heart as we see his care for the floundering church of Galatia. False prophets had crept in and had convinced some to turn from the simplicity of grace, back to the works of the law. In this epistle, Paul counters this dangerous doctrine from every angle. He appeals to the church's logic, to their spiritual experience, and to their previous understanding of the Scriptures.

But in Galatians 4:19, the apostle now appeals to the church through his affection for them. No doubt, the recipients of this letter could hear the tenderness in Paul's voice as they read the words, "My little children, of whom I travail in birth again until Christ be formed in you."

As a pastor, I care about a thousand and one aspects of the church and ministry. I'm interested in the facilities, the landscaping, the websites, the media, the classrooms, the paint, the carpet, the schedule, the bills, the youth activities, the discipleship enrollment—and that's just the beginning! But nothing related to the church is more important to me than seeing Christ formed in each member of our church family.

A true spiritual shepherd carries a profound burden—a burden so heavy that it hurts—for his flock. It is the burning desire of his heart to see them grow in grace.

Real heart labor

Bringing children into the world is, to put it mildly, intense. And it is this intensity of agony that Paul likens to his care for these immature Christians: "My little children, *of whom I travail in birth again* until Christ be formed in you." Paul had already gone through the labor of leading these to Christ and planting a church at Galatia. Yet, he could not be satisfied until he saw the likeness of Christ in their daily living.

In what ways do we travail in ministry? What are these burdens that press against our hearts?

We **travail in the Word.** For a pastor or teacher, diligent study, accurate exegesis, and clear communication of Scripture is *the* primary responsibility. Paul wrote to the young pastor, Timothy, "I charge thee therefore before God, and the Lord Jesus Christ, who shall judge the quick and the dead at his appearing and his kingdom; Preach the word; be instant in season, out of season; reprove, rebuke, exhort with all longsuffering and doctrine" (2 Timothy 4:1–2).

This responsibility is far heavier than that of simple public speaking. There's more to it than just coming up with enough material to fill three sermons a week. It's about knowing the state of the flock and discerning the mind of the Lord for topics. It's about laborious study and preparation along with diligence in a personal walk with the Lord that the message of truth might be communicated purely and freely.

And then there is the **travail through trials**. Those of us who have benefited from others' ministry will never realize the times those others served us while their own hearts were breaking. And those of us who lead other people spiritually understand the weight of ministering to *their* needs while all the time recommitting our own burdens to the Lord. But the trials themselves better equip us to serve; for the trials themselves lead us to the Lord and soften our hearts to the needs of others.

We also **travail in prayer** for those under our care. This travail is perhaps the most fruitful of all—and yet, if we are not careful, it is also the most neglected. Paul could say to Timothy, *without the slightest hint of exaggeration*, "without ceasing I have remembrance of thee in my prayers night and day" (2 Timothy 1:3).

My own prayer life was one of the first areas I, as a young pastor, found sorely lacking. I questioned other pastors about their prayer lives. How did they organize their prayer list? How much time did they pray daily? For all my questions, I found that the best place to learn to pray was on my knees. As I poured out my heart to the Lord and brought the needs of our church family to His throne of grace, I learned that prayer is one of the most intense— and fruitful—labors of a pastor. Paul said of Epaphras that he was "always labouring fervently for you in prayers, that ye may stand perfect and complete in all the will of God" (Colossians 4:12).

Finally, we **travail in oversight**. First Peter 5:2 exhorts pastors, "Feed the flock of God which is among you, taking the oversight thereof, not by constraint, but willingly; not for filthy lucre, but of a ready mind." The oversight of a church is a heavy burden indeed. It was a burden that so pressed Paul that after he presented a condensed list of his physical suffering he wearily added, "Beside those things that are without, that which cometh upon me daily, the care of all the churches" (2 Corinthians 11:28).

Is it any wonder with these types of intense travail that we find that ministry hurts? To deny that ministry hurts would be like a mother denying that her natural birth was painful! But like the mother after labor, we know the end of the pain is bountiful rewards.

These pains of ministry are not only unavoidable for the diligent shepherd, they are commendable. In many ways, they are proof of authenticity and true compassion. But they cannot be shouldered alone. And that is why we who are in ministry need the comforting presence of the Holy Spirit in our lives (John 16:7). He reminds us that Christ "that great shepherd of the sheep" (Hebrews 13:20) carries the burden for us and understands the travail of soul involved in leading others to the likeness of Christ.

The labor I can't do

Labor as we might, there are aspects of the ministry that we simply cannot carry. And that is where we turn a corner on the legitimacy of the hurts of ministry.

Is there a burden of care for Christ's sheep? Absolutely. The more we have the heart of the Good Shepherd, the more we will feel the needs of those to whom we minister.

But here is where our burdens must end. We cannot change a life—only the Holy Spirit can do that. Although we can oversee ministry entrusted to our care, we cannot regulate and control every aspect of its outcome. Some things we must leave to the sovereignty of God.

After all, He is the Burden Bearer; we are simply laborers in His yoke.

The illusion of control

One of the most painful experiences a leader can create for himself is the illusion of control. Frankly, there are *always* circumstances outside of our control. We do not control our own destinies, and—from a perspective of a pastor—we cannot control other people's choices.

Sooner or later, without exception, the illusion of control will produce anxiety. And anxiety is painful. It hinders creativity. It stimulates conflict. It impairs sensitivity to others. It generates "noise" that makes it difficult to hear clearly from the Lord. It's a pain common to those who serve others, but it's avoidable when we realign our perspective to one of faith-filled reality.

Moses couldn't

When out of the burning bush God called Moses to lead His people out of slavery, Moses knew he wasn't equal to the task. It was only after God assured him, reassured him, and finally rebuked his unbelief that Moses submitted to God's calling on his life.

What followed were some of the most spectacular miracles of the Old Testament—the ten plagues of Egypt, the crossing of the Red Sea on dry ground, water out of a rock, bread sent from Heaven. The limitless creative ability of God was displayed in fantastic proportions.

But behind it all was a frazzled Moses, tasked with leading millions of uncongenial, complaining people across the wilderness. At every crisis point, the Israelites laid a load of blame on Moses. And every time they blamed Moses, Moses reminded God how difficult they were to lead. And every time Moses cried out to God, God came through with miraculous splendor.

Apparently the people didn't gripe exclusively about crisis points, and they didn't gripe only to Moses either. They also griped amongst themselves. Their complaints were so prevalent that when Moses' father-in-law, Jethro, came to visit the nation in the wilderness, he found Moses holding and personally presiding over civil court from sunup to sundown. "And it came to pass on the morrow, that Moses sat to judge the people: and the people stood by Moses from the morning unto the evening" (Exodus 18:13).

Although Moses' motives were pure, Jethro pointed out the obvious: "Thou wilt surely wear away, both thou, and this people that is with thee: for this thing is too heavy for thee; thou art not able to perform it thyself alone" (Exodus 18:18). Over the next several verses, Jethro outlined an alternate plan of training and delegation—a plan which Moses wisely adopted, no doubt saving himself from a physical or mental breakdown—or both.

There's something about the combination of our flesh and our desire to serve the Lord that tends to compel us to take on more than is wise or sustainable for the long haul. But as it has been wisely noted, great leaders attribute their success, not primarily to the things they said yes to, but largely to the things they didn't do. To become involved in every ministry opportunity is to break the body and limit the ministry.

I'm a pretty involved sort of person. I'm interested in every aspect of our ministry; and by *every*, I really do mean *every*. Ask my staff. They'll grimace and concur. But I came to a point where I realized I simply don't have to fix every problem. The church is the Lord's, and to acknowledge my limits is to acknowledge His sovereignty.

Be careful where you look

God's callings are always larger than human ability. In calling us to serve others and help to bear their burdens, God enlarges our hearts and stretches our capacities. Sometimes this process of ministry hurts.

Yet, our tendency is to get so enamored with the calling itself that we enlarge the burden that comes with it. We heap pain upon ourselves by assuming added burdens God never intended for us to carry. God calls us to labor in a field larger than our resources so that *He* will get the glory. But we sabotage His glory (and discourage ourselves in the process) when we carry the burden rather than serving in the yoke.

It all boils down to where we look for help when we realize that we are in over our heads. Do we join our voices with the Lifters, echoing their anthem, "Try harder, try harder"? Or do we remember where our help is found?

Paul labored to his limits. He unceasingly invested in people. But he didn't look to himself for strength. Rather he said, "Not that we are sufficient of ourselves to think any thing as of ourselves; but our sufficiency is of God" (2 Corinthians 3:5).

Yes, ministry hurts sometimes. But there's another, greater, yes. Yes, our sufficiency is in God. When we look to Him for our sufficiency, we can labor faithfully and leave the outcomes to Him.

CHAPTER ELEVEN

Depends on How You Look at It

CARRIER PAUSED TO take a breath. He had found himself tiring more easily lately, but suddenly he felt he could go no further. His strength was gone. Not depleted, gone.

Carrier rallied his courage, "Just one more step," he coaxed. But he couldn't take that step. It seemed as though his feet were stuck in the cement beneath him. The yoke, too, seemed extraordinarily heavy. His shoulders stooped beneath its weight.

"Burden Bearer," Carrier whispered, "why aren't You helping me? I can't go further."

"Because you don't need My help now. Carrier, your journey is complete!"

Carrier looked up to an ornate gate before him. Crafted into its intricate design was one beautifully simple word: "Home."

The gate swung open, and Carrier's jaw dropped. What he saw before him was beyond what human language is capable of describing. Beautiful, resplendent, brilliant, magnificent—no, even these adjectives fell short. Strains of the most glorious, melodious music Carrier had ever heard enveloped him in their rich fullness.

As Carrier was lifted through the gate, he realized his yoke was gone. And directly in front of him, riveting the attention of all in this…this *place*, was the Burden Bearer, seated on a splendid throne.

The Burden Bearer smiled a smile of great joy. "Welcome home, Carrier. Well done, thou good and faithful servant."

Carrier had never felt so awestruck or dumbfounded in his entire life. Filled with grateful praise, he searched for words to thank the Burden Bearer.

But his thoughts were interrupted, for just then, Lost Soul from Lifters greeted him. "Thank you, thank you, Carrier, for leading me to Christ."

From the opposite direction, Disciple rushed up to Carrier. "Thank you for taking time to help me grow, Carrier. Thank you for discipling me and teaching me to love and follow the Burden Bearer. Thank you for your example, your time, your care."

As Carrier turned to work his way back through the crowd, Mr. and Mrs. Reunited, hand in hand, greeted him. "Thank you for helping us salvage our marriage." Carrier turned the other direction, but Rowdy Teen stood in his way with a sheepish smile. "Thank you for your time and prayers. Thank you for your patience and for challenging me to grow."

It seemed every direction that Carrier worked to squeeze through the crowd, he was greeted by Lifters—people whose burdens he had sought to carry, people whom he had tried to direct to the Burden Bearer. Some he remembered distinctly, and some he had forgotten. Some had been a chance encounter that Carrier never knew had made any difference at all. But in every case, Carrier hadn't realized the impact which he had on their lives. In fact, sometimes while he had been with them, he had wondered if he was helping them at all! And now they stood crowded, pressing around him, each more eager than the next to express their thanks.

Carrier remembered the pain of the yoke, the blisters on his feet, the weary days and long nights. And they all seemed like nothing to him. It wasn't the chorus of thank you's that brought Carrier such comfort—it was the indescribable joy of seeing all these Lifters here at Home. The Burden Bearer had blessed Carrier's investment in their lives. They stood perfect and complete—the picture of what Carrier had prayed and dreamed for them.

Carrier made another effort to squeeze through the crowd. By now he was almost desperate to reach the Burden Bearer. More than anything he had ever wanted, he wanted to fall at the feet of the Burden Bearer and thank Him.

At last, before the throne, words failed Carrier again.

The Burden Bearer stood. "Well done, my servant, well done." And He placed a crown on Carrier's head.

There was no hesitation now—Carrier's response was more of a reflex than a decision. "Oh, no, Burden Bearer; the crown is Yours." With all the gratitude Carrier had wished he knew how to express, he laid the crown at the Burden Bearer's feet and worshipped His

King: "Thou art worthy, O Lord, to receive glory and honour and power" (Revelation 4:11).

───────────

When the *James Caird* launched from Elephant Island just off the coast of Antarctica, she left twenty-two men waving her Godspeed… and depending upon her soon return.

Originally designed as a mere lifeboat, the *Caird* had already exceeded her carpenter's expectations. The tiny twenty-foot boat had been designed for the ship *Endurance*—the vessel carrying explorers to the first trans-Antarctic expedition, led by Ernest Shackleton. When *Endurance* became ice-locked and then crushed, the twenty-eight-man crew rescued her lifeboats and camped on ice floes for 165 days, praying to drift to land and supplies.

When their last ice pack home broke up in the open sea, the men piled into the three small lifeboats and made a harrowing five-day voyage to Elephant Island. The following morning, Shackleton and a crew of four other men dared against the heaving ocean and set off in their open boat for South Georgia and rescue.

Meanwhile, the twenty-two remaining men turned the two remaining lifeboats into a makeshift hut. Optimistically, they faced two weeks of waiting; realistically, they figured on a month at the longest.

Conditions on the island were miserable, almost unbearable. But the men kept themselves occupied by hunting penguins and seals to stay alive and keeping their "hut," which suffered severe damages with each new storm, livable.

Every morning, a man would trek to the top of the hill and scan the horizon for a relief ship; and every morning he returned disappointed. In the coming weeks the lookout party grew to "most of the men."[1]

Four months after the *Caird* had set sail, one man recorded in his diary, "There is no good in deceiving ourselves any longer."[2] From that point forward, it was a matter of existence. The men hoarded what few personal trinkets had survived their long ordeal and did their best to make themselves comfortable. The hut saw minor improvements, and the men continued their daily trip to the lookout bluff. That trip, however, was more of a ritual than an expectation. There could be no hope that the small *Caird* had survived.

But, on August 30, 1916, a ship was spotted a mile off shore. The men couldn't signal it in fast enough. Rushing to the icy shore, the men strained to see their rescue ship. Shackleton himself, having braved a heroic journey against incredible odds, greeted the castaways and urged them to hurry onboard.

In that moment, four months and six days evaporated as twenty-two men rejoiced in their rescue. Without hesitation or disappointment, they hurried onto the ship, happily leaving behind their makeshift hut and the personal trinkets that just hours earlier had seemed so precious. Their perspective transformed, they looked now only toward the comfort and joy aboard that ship.

That's how it will be with us. I believe that when you and I enter eternity, our perspective will change. The comfort which we so thoroughly seek now and the possessions (or relationships or accomplishments or status or opportunities) which we so carefully guard, will seem like nothing. That which seemed so burdensome and painful on Earth will evaporate into sheer glory. Without hesitation or disappointment, we'll happily leave it all behind and rejoice in the physical presence of the Burden Bearer.

Perspective

Although Carrier's entrance into Heaven was described above with imaginative license, I'm quite certain it wasn't embellished. Heaven is beyond our fondest expectations and wildest dreams. I'm pretty sure that once we enter, we'll gasp and say, "I could never have imagined!"

The only problem is that we *can't* see Heaven now. So is our only option to toil on in grief and misery? How are we to view the heavy burdens and long-lasting trials that we carry now?

Second Corinthians 4:17–18 encourages us to remember that it is a matter of perspective: "For our light affliction, which is but for a moment, worketh for us a far more exceeding and eternal weight of glory; While we look not at the things which are seen, but at the things which are not seen: for the things which are seen are temporal; but the things which are not seen are eternal."

One author reminded, "Even our most painful experience in life is but a temporary setback. Our pain and suffering may or may not be relieved in this life, but they will certainly be relieved in the next. That is Christ's promise—no more death or pain; He will wipe away all our tears. He took our sufferings on Himself so that one day He might remove all suffering from us. That is the biblical foundation for our optimism. No Christian should be a pessimist. We should be realists—focused on the reality that we serve a sovereign and gracious God. *Because of the reality of Christ's atoning sacrifice and his promises, biblical realism is optimism*" (emphasis mine).[3]

Calibrate the scales

If you were to describe your trials and heartaches, what words would you use? *Heavy? Permanent?*

The Lord must have a different scale and timeline than we do, because He describes them as *light* and *but for a moment*. He doesn't choose these words because He is callused to our pain. He isn't making light of our suffering or ignoring our needs.

He is reminding us to view our burdens in light of eternity.

Compared to the weight of glory awaiting us in Heaven, the weight of our present suffering is light. To a child, one hundred pounds may be heavy, but weighed against a 100-ton loaded railcar, it won't even tip the scale.

Compared to the length of eternity, the duration of our pain *is* momentary. To a child, an hour may seem like forever, but calculated on a clock that counts millennia, it doesn't even move the hands.

When God tells us that our affliction is short and light, He is reminding us to recalibrate our measurements to eternal scales. He is encouraging us to look past our immediate feelings and experiences and choose to see our pain through the eyes of faith.

Paul made this choice when he said, "For I reckon that the sufferings of this present time are not worthy to be compared with the glory which shall be revealed in us" (Romans 8:18).

Through these words, the Lord parts the backstage curtain and allows us a glimpse into the stage of eternity. What we endure today, any pain associated with yoke-bearing, will be richly repaid. The benefits of the heaviness we endure today will be enjoyed for *eternity*—a word too large and too long for us to wrap our minds around.

Why we don't faint

Eternity may be long, but let's face it—it also seems far away. Yes, we have the promise of heavenly benefits, but we also have the presence of the cares of this life. They wear on us. They deplete our energy. They empty our reserves.

What is it that keeps us going this side of eternity? How are we sustained through the journey?

Two words: inner man.

What Scripture refers to as the "inner man" is the core of our soul—our spirit which the Burden Bearer renews solely by His presence.

"For which cause we faint not; but though our outward man perish, yet the inward man is renewed day by day" (2 Corinthians 4:16).

Our outward man is a mere "earthen vessel"—a frail and failing container that displays the power of God within (2 Corinthians 4:7). But our inward man is renewable.

Everything—*everything*—can be falling apart with the outward man, and yet the inward man can sustain us to the finish line. Paul knew this. Notice how he contrasted the very real calamities experienced by the outward man with the sustaining power in the inner man: "We are troubled on every side, yet not distressed; we are perplexed, but not in despair; Persecuted, but not forsaken; cast down, but not destroyed" (2 Corinthians 4:8–9).

Yes, the inward man keeps us going.

If—and it's an important if—the inner man is kept renewed by God.

You see, the inner man is the part of us that can be nourished and strengthened *only* by God. This is why Paul prayed for the Christians at Ephesus, "That he would grant you, according to the riches of his glory, to be strengthened with might by his Spirit in the inner man" (Ephesians 3:16).

We can rally another person's courage; we can incite his enthusiasm; we can renew hope in his mind. But when it comes to the inner man, only God's Spirit can strengthen the deepest part of our being.

Obviously then, the greatest mistake we make is to neglect the inner man—to share Christ's yoke while never seeking strength from Him. But that's exactly what we're prone to do. We look to Christian friends, great books, wise speakers, and even our social media stream to provide encouragement and spiritual strength.

And inasmuch as these sources use Scripture, they can provide a degree of strength.

But when we have reached the end of our strength, when the outward man has gone one step past exhaustion, we will wish we had been looking to the Holy Spirit to strengthen the inner man all along.

Serving in the yoke with Christ includes many possible distractions from the inner man. It's easy to become so engaged in the lives of others and in the service of the Burden Bearer that we neglect nourishing our inner man.

And yet, if we are to maintain an eternal perspective, if we are to labor strong until the finish line, if we are to grow in our love for and understanding of the Burden Bearer, we have one choice: nourish the inner man. Spend time in God's Word, surrender to the Holy Spirit, cultivate a relationship with the Lord.

Take the long view

Ophthalmologists call it *myopia*, but most of us call it *nearsightedness*. I call it "I need my glasses!" Without my glasses, I don't see far. At least, I don't see far very clearly.

We Lifters are beset with spiritual myopia. Even when we cultivate the skills of long-range planning and mature in the practice of looking years down the road in our decision making, our forward thinking rarely penetrates into eternity.

We so easily forget that today's yoke will be transformed into tomorrow's crown. We see our afflictions, and we lose hope. Or complain. Or wrestle. Or faint.

But should we look at our afflictions through the lenses of God's promises, we see them for what they really are—momentary and light. And best of all, they are working for us an eternal weight of glory.

Do we have pain? Yes. Do we grieve as we bear the burdens of others? Yes.

But how do we see that pain, that grief? Well, it all depends on how you look at it.

May we choose to look beyond today's suffering and, peering into eternity, rejoice in our certain rewards.

It is the forward joy of every Lifter—the day when the Burden Bearer says, "Well done." And we, almost as a reflex, reply, "Thou art worthy!"

---

1.   Alfred Lansing, *Endurance* (Basic Books, 2007), 215.

2.   Ibid.

3.   Randy Alcorn, *Heaven* (Tyndale House Publishers, Inc., 2004), 444.

CONCLUSION TO PART 3

THROUGH THESE PAGES, we've come full circle. From struggling to balance our own burdens to committing to labor with Christ to serving with Him to bear the burdens of others, we've grown in our understanding of the Burden Bearer and His willingness to carry our loads.

As we conclude this book, I encourage you to take a moment to review what we have just learned in part three about our service for the Burden Bearer. As you serve in His yoke, are you submitting to His pace—learning to rest? Are you finding your strength through His grace and taking the opportunity to pass on that grace to others? Are you leaving the unknown and the unexplainable aspects of your journey to the trust of His wise sovereignty? Are you gladly choosing to be spent for others while leaving the responsibility for the outcome to the Lord? And finally, are you purposefully maintaining an eternal perspective?

Perhaps as you reflect on these aspects of serving Christ, you feel the need for adjustments and growth. Thankfully, when Christ offered us His yoke, He included the invitation, "Learn of Me." May we do just that—learn of the Burden Bearer as we walk with Him.

Personal Reflections

_____

_____

_____

_____

_____

_____

_____

_____

_____

_____

_____

_____

_____

_____

_____

_____

_____

_____

The Impossible Burden

BEFORE WE WERE even old enough to know it, we Lifters had a tremendous—actually, an *impossible*—burden weighing down our souls. In fact, this burden is the most grievous weight we will ever carry. Although we don't always recognize that the burden is there, it is. And it has disastrous consequences. Let me explain.

Why the Burden Bearer came

Jesus didn't come to Earth some two thousand years ago just to encourage us or provide a good example. He—God in the flesh (1 Timothy 3:15)—came because we were strapped with the incredible, awful burden of sin. We were all born with a sin nature that separates us from God. Romans 3:23 explains, "For all have sinned, and come short of the glory of God." Even the best of us are sinners.

Sin has a high price tag, too. Romans 6:23 says, "For the wages of sin is death...." In other words, the price for sin is eternal death, apart from God, in a lake of fire called Hell. Revelation 21:8 describes this place and those who go there: "But the fearful, and unbelieving, and the abominable, and murderers, and whoremongers, and sorcerers, and idolaters, and all liars, shall have their part in the lake which burneth with fire and brimstone: which is the second death." Literally, this is where sinners (like you and me) are headed, apart from the miracle of Christ and what He provided for us.

A burden too big for human answers

Many people—both religious and non-religious alike—have misconceptions as to what we can do to rid ourselves of the burden of sin. Some believe that simply being "born into a Christian family" does the trick. Others claim that if we do enough good works—give enough money, share enough kindness, love enough people, have a high enough standard of morality, or any number of "enough" whatevers—that this will at least make our good outweigh our burden of sin. Still others believe it has nothing to do with religion and that God only judges the sincerity of our hearts. They maintain that if we are sincere and consistent in our chosen belief system, He will overlook our faults.

But think about it: all of these suggestions to rid ourselves of the sin burden boil down to the same answer—"try harder."

But, we've just seen that we can't try hard enough. In vivid imagery, God tells us just how serious the problem is: "But we are all as an unclean thing, and all our righteousnesses are as filthy rags" (Isaiah 64:6). Try as hard as we can, even the best things we do cannot begin to compare to the holiness of God.

We need a better answer. We need a Burden Bearer.

And that is why Jesus came. He didn't just come to help us with our emotional, relational, financial, and physical burdens. He came to relieve us of the weightiest burden of all—the burden of sin. Mark 10:45 tells us, "the Son of man came…to give his life a ransom for many."

How the Burden Bearer did the impossible

When Jesus voluntarily died on the cross, the Bible says that He "bare our sins in his own body on the tree" (1 Peter 2:24). As we saw a moment ago, the payment for our sin is death, but in God's great mercy, Jesus made that payment for us. In Romans 5:8 God says, "But God commendeth [demonstrated] his love toward us, in that, while we were yet sinners, Christ died for us." Our payment for sin is *death*; and Jesus *died* in our place!

Jesus Christ came to Earth as God in the flesh, lived a perfect life, and then gave His life because He loves you. On that cross, He literally paid for all of your sins. He took your blame! He punished

Himself for your sin. Then, because He is God, He rose from the dead three days later.

John 3:16 says, "For God so loved the world, that he gave his only begotten Son, that whosoever believeth in him should not perish, but have everlasting life." God, in His awesome love, came to Earth to make a way for you to be forgiven of your sins and given eternal life!

Release your burden

Knowing that Jesus bore your sins is not enough. You must trust Him to take your burden of sin. It's a personal decision.

God uses the analogy of a gift. The last half of Romans 6:23 says, "...but the gift of God is eternal life through Jesus Christ our Lord." A gift must be purchased, *and* it must be received. To have your burden of sin released, you must receive God's gift—the gift of eternal life. Romans 10:13 says, "For whosoever shall call upon the name of the Lord shall be saved." In verse 10 of that same chapter, God says, "For with the heart man believeth unto righteousness; and with the mouth confession is made unto salvation." It's as simple as believing what God says and then choosing to receive His gift!

If you've never asked Jesus Christ to be your personal Saviour, you could do that right now. Simply confess to Him that you understand you are a sinner deserving of Hell and that you trust His payment for your forgiveness and salvation. You could sincerely pray something like this:

Lord Jesus, I believe that You are God, that You died for my sin, and that You rose again from the dead. I know that I am a sinner, and I ask You now to be my personal Saviour. I'm placing my full trust in You alone, and I now accept Your gift of eternal life. Thank You for keeping Your promise!

Knowing the Burden Bearer personally starts right here, with this decision. When you meet Him at the cross, trusting His payment for your sins, you then have direct access to Him in seeking His help for every other burden you face.

If you have just now chosen to receive Christ's gift, I would love to hear from you! Please send an email to BurdenBearer@ strivingtogether.com. Additionally, you will find resources and Bible messages to help you grow in your relationship with God at our website: paulchappell.com.

ABOUT THE AUTHOR

DR. PAUL CHAPPELL is the senior pastor of Lancaster Baptist Church and the president of West Coast Baptist College in Lancaster, California. He is a powerful communicator of God's Word and a passionate servant to God's people. He has been married to his wife, Terrie, since 1980, and they have four married children who are all serving in Christian ministry. He enjoys spending time with his family and serving the Lord shoulder to shoulder with a wonderful church family.

Dr. Chappell's preaching is heard on Daily in the Word, a radio program that is broadcast across America. You can find a station listing at paulchappell.com/radio.

You can also connect with Dr. Chappell here:

Blog: paulchappell.com
Twitter: twitter.com/paulchappell
Facebook: facebook.com/pastor.paul.chappell

BOOKS WE THINK YOU WILL LOVE...

Renew By Paul Chappell

90 Days of Spiritual Refreshment

This ninety-day devotional guide will encourage you to seek God's face and renew your heart in His Word. Each devotion includes a Scripture passage and provides an encouraging or admonishing truth regarding your walk with the Lord.

Time Out for Parents By Paul Chappell

90 Days of Biblical Encouragement

The ninety devotions in this book are written to encourage parents to seek God's wisdom as they raise their children for Him. At the close of each devotion is a single actionable thought given as "Today's Parenting Principle."

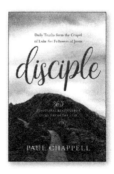

Disciple By Paul Chappell

Daily Truths from the Gospel of Luke for Followers of Jesus

Each daily reading in Disciple will take you on a journey through the Gospel of Luke and the chronological account of the life of Christ. As these brief devotions draw you closer to the Lord, you'll be challenged and encouraged to follow Jesus more closely and to walk with Him each day.

STRIVINGTOGETHER.COM

ALSO AVAILABLE AS EBOOKS

BOOKS WE THINK YOU WILL LOVE...

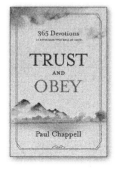

Trust and Obey By Paul Chappell
365 Devotions to Encourage Your Walk of Faith

Paul Chappell's Trust and Obey devotional will encourage your spiritual growth. The readings conclude with a solid takeaway principle which you can apply to your life immediately. You'll be challenged and encouraged to follow Jesus more closely and to walk with Him in practical ways throughout each day.

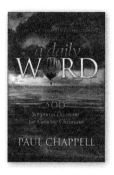

A Daily Word By Paul Chappell
366 Scriptural Devotions for Growing Christians

Designed to complement your daily devotional walk with the Lord, this book from Dr. Paul Chappell features 366 daily devotional thoughts to strengthen and encourage your spiritual life. Each devotion features a one-year Bible reading selection.

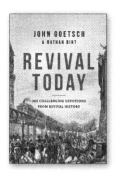

Revival Today By John Goetsch & Nathan Birt
365 Challenging Devotions from Revival History

Each devotion in this book is written to encourage you that revival is still possible today. Each daily reading describes an event or individual from the past that God has used to bring revival.

STRIVINGTOGETHER.COM
ALSO AVAILABLE AS EBOOKS

BOOKS WE THINK YOU WILL LOVE...

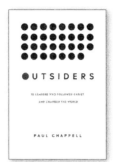

Outsiders By Paul Chappell
15 Leaders Who Followed Christ and Changed the World

Discover fifteen leaders from history who followed Christ and changed the world. Their testimonies will stir your faith, strengthen your commitment, and renew your dedication to Christ.

Are We There Yet? By Paul & Terrie Chappell

Marriage—The Perfect Journey for Imperfect Couples

This book is for every couple at any stage of the marriage journey. It will help reveal a God-given perspective that can change and strengthen your marriage. A companion guide is sold separately.

Making Home Work in a Broken Society By Paul Chappell

Bible Principles for Raising Children and Building Families

God has entrusted you, as a parent, to care for and raise your children for Him—but it's not easy. Discover what it means to invest in your children and how you can bring them up in the nurture and admonition of the Lord.

STRIVINGTOGETHER.COM
ALSO AVAILABLE AS EBOOKS